BUCKSKIN JOE

Buckskin Joe

being the unique and vivid memoirs of
Edward Jonathan Hoyt
hunter-trapper, scout, soldier, showman,
frontiersman, and friend of the Indians
1840–1918

Taken from his Original Manuscript and Notes
and Edited by
GLENN SHIRLEY

UNIVERSITY OF NEBRASKA PRESS · LINCOLN

First Bison Book printing: 1988
Most recent printing indicated by the first digit below:
1   2   3   4   5   6   7   8   9   10

Library of Congress Cataloging-in-Publication Data

Hoyt, Edward Jonathan, 1840–1918.
   Buckskin Joe: being the unique and vivid memoirs
of Edward Jonathan Hoyt, hunter-trapper, scout, soldier, showman, frontiersman, and friend of the Indians, 1840–1918 / taken from his original manuscript
and notes and edited by Glenn Shirley.
        p.   cm.
   Includes index.
   ISBN 0-8032-7239-1 (pbk.)
   1. Hoyt, Edward Jonathan, 1840–1918.
2. Pioneers—West (U.S.)—Biography. 3. Frontier
and pioneer life—West (U.S.) 4. West (U.S.)—History—1848–1950. 5. Circus—United States. 6.
United States—History—Civil War, 1861–1865—
Personal narratives.
I. Shirley, Glenn. II. Title.
F594.H8   1988
978′.02′0924—dc19
[B]   CIP 87-27364

For his living grandson—

DR. VANCE JOSEPH HOYT

"Buckskin Joe, Jr."

Preface

In writing *Pawnee Bill*, the biography of Major Gordon W. Lillie, White Chief of the Pawnees, last of the land boomers and Wild West showman, I touched upon the lives of many American pioneers, both deceased and living, who were associated with him in the settlement of the West and his later efforts to preserve and depict the life of an era the world will never again witness. I was amazed at how many of these people felt that their early experiences should have been written and saved.

Consequently, I was not surprised when Dr. Vance Joseph Hoyt, of Topanga, California, modestly offered to me the reminiscences of his grandfather, Edward Jonathan Hoyt, known on the plains for more than forty years as "Buckskin Joe." "Gramp jotted down a few sketches," he said. "If they could be of any use to you, I would be glad."

I had mentioned Joe's career only briefly in the Lillie biography. From Lillie's Wild West show records, I had learned that he was a native of Canada, Province of Quebec, where he won his name in the early 1850's as a hunter and trapper among the Northwest Indians. He showed a talent early for music, mastering, in all, sixteen instruments, but chiefly the violin and the cornet. He organized and directed a number of bands and orchestras, achieving distinction as the first "Border Musician" and acquiring the title of "Professor." Later, he worked as an aerial performer and acrobat and traveled with some of the first steamboat and wagon circuses to tour the eastern and central United States.

At the outbreak of the Civil War, he enlisted in the Union army. This was the beginning of an honorable and varied service to his adopted country. Joe fought with the Army of the Potomac under General George B. McClellan and in so many battles that he "lost track of them." When the war ended, he came west to fight Indians.

He was one of the first men to settle in southern Kansas on the present site of Arkansas City, and the next twenty years made the town headquarters for his many expeditions into Indian Territory and the Rockies.

During the silver strikes of 1879, he went to Leadville, Colorado, where he sank twenty-two mining shafts, survived several brushes with claim jumpers, and served as trouble-shooter for Horace A. W. "Haw" Tabor, Colorado's "Silver King." He explored the Western Slope and Ute Indian country, and was there during the Ute uprising and the Meeker Massacre. Today a gulch near Aspen and a rebuilt mining town near Canon City bear his name.

From 1880 to 1883, Joe guided immigrants across the plains to Colorado and the Western Slope. He searched for gold in Nova Scotia during 1884, returning to Kansas a year later. In 1888, he entered the show business with Pawnee Bill, and the next year made the "land rush" into Oklahoma. From 1890 to 1891, he served as deputy United States marshal for the District of Kansas and Oklahoma Territory, then re-entered the show life and played the country with his own Buckskin Joe Wild West aggregation, until seized again with the "gold fever" in 1897.

His last and greatest expedition was into the jungles of Honduras, where he worked an old Spanish mine for four years before being caught up in a revolution and forced to flee the country, badly wounded and leaving behind valuable discoveries from which others profited. In 1909, he disposed of his interests in Kansas and Oklahoma and moved to California. He died at Los Angeles on April 20, 1918.

"Gramp's and Gordon Lillie's lives were interlocked in many ways, and your *Pawnee Bill* is so closely authentic to the events I still remember," Dr. Hoyt told me, "that I decided you were the person to do the life of Buckskin Joe." He placed in my hands heavy boxes of old photographs, a bulky scrapbook, Wild West show and circus records, a Civil War diary, mining documents, and Joe's penciled notes. I did not realize until I had examined them that his grandfather had written a book. I wrote Dr. Hoyt at once and told him I wished to prepare the manuscript for publication over his grandfather's name. He was pleased and willing for me to handle it as desired.

Joe's original manuscript is arranged frequently without regard for chronology or outline. In addition, many of the events he describes are in separate articles and only briefly mentioned in the original; his Civil War years, for example, are detailed in his diary running from 1859 through 1864, and the account of his expedition into Central America appears in a series of lengthy letters written from his camp in the Southern Mountains of the Olancho District, Honduras, and published in the Oklahoma City *Times Journal*, March 16 through August 18, 1898.

Consequently, I reorganized much of his material so that it would read as a connected narrative, integrated his side articles which gave greater detail to an otherwise sketchy reference to certain happenings, deleted several events which he described but in which he did not participate and which I felt were irrelevant, and changed the actual wording only where the grammar and phraseology were hopelessly obscure. In short, despite what overhauling I did, the sentences are still his—his words, his style, anecdotes, remarks, criticisms, and interpretations of the times and the people. I did not feel that his sometimes blatant jargon should be tampered with. It is as much a part of his character as his long hair and buckskin regalia. I enjoy the flavor it imparts.

Several passages in his narrative required additional information and historical verification; this information I have enclosed in brackets. Believing that history is an art as well as compilation and should be presented as a story of living people, I have purposely avoided the use of footnotes, and have added the bracketed information only as it could be incorporated to clarify and explain without slowing the narrrative.

The intimate details of the day-to-day life of those hardy folk who crossed the Mississippi seeking a new life and fortunes are seldom recorded in books on the opening of the West. Edward Jonathan Hoyt presents them here with photographic accuracy, salty humor, and a shrewd judgment of his contemporaries, without the usual Wild West type of glamour. Basically a story of toil and hardship, it is most of all an account of one man's attempt to enjoy life in all its various manifestations and his raw courage to dare be unpredictable.

I hope other readers enjoy it as much as I did.

Stillwater, Oklahoma   GLENN SHIRLEY

Contents

Contents

A picture section follows page 114.

BUCKSKIN JOE

CHAPTER I

From the Cradle into the Woods

At 6 P.M., October 4, 1840, I came kicking and squalling into the world in a log cabin under the shadow of old Mt. Orford near the village of Magog, Lower Canada, now the Province of Quebec. The country was wilderness then, inhabited by Indians and animals of the forest. People were few and far between, wild, woolly, and uncouth, but honest lovers of good whiskey and athletic sports. The wrestling ring, old town ball, running and skating matches, the hop and kick, and rifle shooting, the test and standard of the men—these and dancing were the principal amusements. Those were the days when whistlers were in demand. A man who could sit up all night and whistle for dancing, just for the pleasure and honor of being a little better whistler than the other fellow, was considered something extra.

When a young man married, it was the custom for everybody to turn out for a house warming—build him a house out of logs with a puncheon floor [logs hewed on three sides and wedged tightly together]—and start a dance, always with enough grub and good whiskey to keep all hands happy and the head musician, the whistler, going for two or three days. One more entertainment and the young couple were ready to become full-fledged denizens of the forest. This was called a log-rolling bee. A piece of land was cleared and the cut brush and timber rolled into huge

1

piles for burning, leaving the land around the stumps for cultivation.

I have heard my mother tell how Grandfather Hoyt and my Uncle Acey postponed a big hunt just for the purpose of ascertaining my sex. When it was announced that I was a boy, they shouted and danced, and Grandfather let out a big yell: "That's the kind! May he live long and prosper. Hurry up, Acey—we will have bear meat for him when we come back."

My father, Samuel Hoyt, had left home when he was a young man and traveled with his pack on his back to Boston, Massachusetts, to see the city and do business on his own account. He worked on the railroad that was being built in the country between Lowell and Boston, about 1832, then got a job as night watchman at a glass factory and remained six years. During that time he took violin and dancing lessons. Finally he married a young widow, Mrs. Judith Sampson Hugins Danforth, mother of one child, Ellen, who was left in Medford to be raised by an uncle, Benjamin Sampson, a ship builder. Mother was the daughter of an old sea captain who had lost large cargos in the Atlantic, which came near unbalancing his mind. He was caught in the act of shooting himself barely in time to save his life.

Father returned at once to his home in Canada with his new wife and took charge of Grandfather's estate in the wilderness. He set up housekeeping in a log cabin which Grandfather had erected for a school house, a little too soon for the neighborhood at the time, but it came in good play and answered all requirements in ushering me into existence. I was christened Edward Jonathan, a name I used little afterwards.

Father was the first fiddler in the country and in great demand. He soon erected a large house with a long hall overhead, and he and Mother, both good dancers, gave lessons during the winter and held quarterly balls. Though whiskey was the common beverage, Father was a teetotaler in the extreme, and Mother was always opposed to drunkenness, rowdyism, and many of the rude customs which have passed. I can only swear allegiance to her when I say that, although the rod was the order of the day and came down heavy upon all sides for boyish pranks, her kind and gentle influence could hold my restless spirit far better than the birch stick. On the other hand, her city accomplishments tended not a little to relieve the monotony. She was a great mimic and actress. I have not found in natural talent her equal. She would dress in a sailor suit and dance the Sailor's Hornpipe to the astonishment of the natives.

Although she came from Boston, she proved her fitness for backwoods life. She took her place as helpmate to my father, milking the cows, feeding the pigs, and all the outdoor work which women of those early days found necessary in carving a new country from the wilderness.

Which brings me to my first grip with danger. Still in swaddling clothes, I took little part in the adventure except to give the alarm that a one-year-old could muster through his lungs.

Mother had gone to do the evening milking, leaving me in my cradle. My cries brought her on the double, the milking stool in her hand. A wild hog had quietly entered the cabin and was running into the woods with her baby boy in its mouth. During the chase, about to collapse in despair, she flung the stool. The hog squealed and so did I. The hog escaped with part of my clothing in its snout, leaving the subject of this narrative for further action by land and sea.

Again, when I was only a month older and Mother was out doing chores, a burning coal snapped from our big fireplace and lodged under the quilts in my cradle. I gave one of my hideous yells, which brought Mother on the run to find me enveloped in flames, and in the nick of time to save me.

Life passed with the usual occurrences until I was three. One winter day, becoming highly offended at my parents, I ran away barefooted two miles in the snow to my old grandfather's cabin on Castle Brook, and was received with open arms by my grandmother, a good old Scotch lady, about as follows: "God bless my boy. God bless those little toes. How did you ever get here? Come set by the fire while I get something to eat."

You can bet I was first at the table. The old lady was a great

3

admirer of pluck and courage. Grandfather was a great lover of whiskey and administered enough to his pet to elevate him. I have a faint recollection of then going to a neighbor named Gunstell and being turned away. After wading the mud in his cattle pen, I made for home, and on greeting my mother by a sudden entrance head foremost, slipped, struck the woodbox with my nose, and lay sprawled on the floor. You can imagine Mother's job before she got me to bed.

Next came the golden days, the same in the lives of all boys of all nations, with one exception—in my time the rod was the supreme and controlling power.

A schoolhouse had been built near Ward's Corner, about a half mile from home. I didn't learn much. Books seemed to be out of my line. I spent most of my time jumping out the window to escape punishment. Once during recess I killed a huge snake, and being the last one inside, I stretched it across the doorstep. When recess for the girls was called, the fun commenced. Every girl screamed and jumped the steps. They reminded me of sheep scampering a stone wall. The teacher had no trouble discovering the guilty one, but I was out the window again before she reached me.

Finally the school board paid the schoolma'am a visit, complaining that she did not use the rod enough. I was invited to step forward. A birch stick was plied most vigorously while I kept time bounding up and down on top of the woodbox. The blows descended until the stick and schoolma'am were worn out. My back was cut in several places and my clothing stained with blood, but not a tear nor yelp came from me. When she had finished, I thanked her kindly, kicked the stovepipe down, tore the door off its hinges, and left—only to get another licking when I got home.

This caused an invisible power to take possession of my body which I could never account for. I could not control my limbs— my gait was two steps forward and one backwards. Despite all I could do, this had to be done. It took utmost persistence to conquer it, and for a long time afterward I could not get my hands into my pockets without struggling as if I was going to have a fit. I remember in spelling class one day trying to get my hands into my pockets and working with such energy the schoolma'am became frightened and sent me home. Mother laughed for she had seen the performance before. But I didn't go back to school for a while.

I began to ride horses and trap on Cherry River. I was permitted to hunt and fish and acquire my first experiences of a wild life which was heaven to me and the height of my ambition. My cousin, Alonzo, and myself would go three miles to the lake at the mouth of Cherry River and watch the camp at night while the men went out in the boat equipped with jack and spear. My father was spearsman and Uncle Acey served as paddler with jack in the center to burn pitch pine for light to reflect in the water to see the fish. The fish lay on the bottom of the lake where they congregated in the fall and multiplied. Sometimes they were so thick we could spear them with a pitchfork.

Here I learned to spear and paddle my own canoe. It took steady nerves, strong arms, and nice calculation to spear fish by the light of a torch at nighttime. Here, too, I received my first lesson in gunning. One day I stole Uncle Acey's flint musket and went after big game. I found a squirrel instead. I poked the old gun through a fence, took aim, and pulled the trigger. The charge went one way, I another, and the gun straight up; and the squirrel, God only knows where, for I never went back to find out.

This experience, however, did not cure my hunter's instinct. Father had a very misbehaved bull that he kept tied in the barn. One morning I placed our tomcat on the bull's back to see what would happen. Almost at once things took on a lively disposition. The bull pitched and bellowed, and the more he capered, the harder old Thomas hung on with his claws. I was standing at the rear enjoying the show when the old fellow let drive with one foot, sending me through the side of the barn. The bull broke loose, tearing down his stall, and leaped over me under the pile of boards. When Father appeared on the scene, the situation was such as to demand an explanation. Boylike, I informed him that, while passing, the old devil got mad and kicked me through the wall. I never mentioned the cat. Old Thomas wouldn't have figured well in the narrative I had concocted.

So father put His Majesty on pasture, surrounded by a high stake fence. The next time I went hunting, I decided to cut through the pasture to conserve a bit of energy. If the bull took after me, I intended to shoot him. But when he came bellowing my direction, I did not find time to shoot. I broke for the fence, threw my gun over, and just as I started to jump the old fellow rendered such assistance that I landed several feet on the other side. Furious, I grabbed my gun, shoved it through the fence and, just as the bull turned, gave him the contents in the rear. He whirled, tail erect, and retreated—the first time he had been bested in his life. The next time Father went around him with a big stick, he turned and ran. Father couldn't understand it. He asked me, "What have you been doing to that bull?"

"Not much," I said. "I found the right medicine and gave it to him." Then I ventured to tell him how I had been forced to jump the fence to save my life. "As he turned, I gave him a charge in the rear."

"Yes," said Father, "you might have put out his eyes."

"I do not think so," said I, "for I knew which end to shoot."

About this time a circus came to town. My oldest brother, Albert, and Warren, who was several years younger, had never seen a circus. I arranged with Mother for money for them and myself, and we lit out for a three-mile run to the village. It was all Warren could do to keep up with Albert and me. At last we topped the hill overlooking the showgrounds. First, we took in everything that was free outside as our capital was limited. The band began playing and inside we scampered, climbing to the highest seat we could find. The round-topped tent was only sixty feet in diameter, but things looked mighty big to us. The old clown was the funniest man we had ever seen. Our eyes never left him, and we watched eagerly every motion he made. I knew I could repeat them precisely. When I got home, I practiced every trick and ditty he had performed. This was the beginning of my circus career.

The clown had performed one trick with a cigar. It was the most difficult one for me, for I had never smoked a cigar. But I was doing it up fine, when suddenly I felt something wrong inside. I went in the house to eat supper. This was necessary. If I failed to eat, things would look mistrusty for me. I wasn't ready for an explanation, so I sat down and commenced. A moment later, I leaped from my chair and made for the door. Father demanded to know what was wrong, but I was too busy to explain. In those days the slightest variation in a boy's habits always necessitated unpleasantness from the head of the family, and father was no exception. He always came out ahead and I came out behind. At least that is where I suffered the most.

During these years I received my first impressions of religion. There was a meeting going on near our place where they claimed the world was coming to an end and that all such chaps as myself would be burned in hellfire. I think those good people were in earnest, but I could not understand such rolling and tumbling and shrieking. At one meeting I attended with Uncle Acey, he became so disgusted that he rose to his feet, and in a voice that sounded like thunder, shouted: "You are all a set of darn fools. Come, Bud"—as he called me—"Let's go home." And the preacher began shouting to the crowd, "Pray for Acey! Pray for Acey!"

It was amusing to me, for I had no faith in this world coming to an end prophecy. Life seemed too interesting to end so abruptly.

It had been announced that many were to be baptized Sunday morning at Castle Brook bridge. The river was frozen over and it occurred to me how I could have a little fun. I fixed it with Alonzo's sister, a buxom girl of sixteen, who was a good swimmer and one of those to be baptized. I stood on the bridge in such glory that I must have been baptized by the unholy devil. The minister and my cousin walked into the water where the ice had been cut out. When the skinny preacher doused her, she screamed and grabbed him around the neck according to the program, and under they went. The cold water roiled and foamed and some

7

of the people got excited and rushed to the rescue. But that cousin of mine—a mighty plucky girl!—grabbed them around the neck also, and such yelling and excitement I never seen. I knew better than to manifest my pleasure. I was looked upon with distrust anyway. But I enjoyed it greatly, for I did not like this minister, and he sure got the ducking of his life.

There was another sort of religious order called the Rackensacks that met in the attic of our house. My father was ringleader, and I was quite curious to know what they did up there—everything was so secret. One day I stole the keys and unlocked the big box where they kept their paraphernalia, and discovered things I hadn't dreamed of—an old saw they used for a gong, white robes, a skull and crossbones. I rushed downstairs and informed Mother. She was in for the fun as much as myself. We put on the robes and had a ghost dance that lasted several hours. Their initiation must have been a hideous affair. Anyone who passed muster must have remembered it for some time. When Father came home that evening and found out what I had done, I got something that I remembered for a while.

Besides the Rackensacks, Father was interested in perpetual motion. He had made a large drum about five feet tall and two feet in diameter, with tin tubes projecting from the sides in all directions. Each tube was filled with lead balls that rolled about like shot in capsules, causing the tube to revolve. Once started, it would rotate for days. The noise was terrible. But we all had to stand it for it was perpetual motion. Finally the thing would run down and give us a rest.

I now took the trail with my grandfather, trapping, hunting, and fishing. It brought me in contact with squawmen, half-breeds, and full-blooded Indians. This was his life, and I was with him whenever I could compromise with Father through Mother and get away. We carried our provisions, blankets, and camp outfit on our backs. Grandfather was a small man, but one of the most wiry and enduring I ever knew. Few men ever put him on his back. He was full of fun and stories, and always let me carry the gun. It took from one to two weeks to go out and back on our line of traps. We went out in the fall when the woods begin to turn and the earth to prepare for her winter sleep. I would look up at the stars from our bed of pine boughs and listen to the cries of wild animals all about us, without fear. Grandfather taught me never to fear anything in the wilderness.

We would follow the hardwood ridges out and come back along the streams. The ridges we called "sable lines," and we caught these weasellike creatures in deadfalls set with a figure four. We set deadfalls for bear and mink, and steel traps for other fur-bearing animals. We trapped for otter and beaver in the streams. It took skill and close observation. Otter would abandon their slides on the first discovery of fresh sign, so we had to keep away from the banks. We built a raft and went up or down the streams, setting our traps under water. The traps, stakes and chains were always concealed a little distance from the shore to keep the otter from gnawing off their legs when caught to escape. But bear, mink, and sable would poke their noses into any place to get something to eat. Sometimes we would drag a sheep's head to coax them in line for our traps.

Once we came upon a black bear caught in one of our deadfalls. The weight not being heavy enough to hold him down, he was making things fly lively and tearing up the earth in general. Grandfather had the ax and I had the gun, and just as the bear broke out of the trap, Grandfather shouted: "Stand aside, Bud!" He made a pass with the ax, but the old bear knocked it out of his hands with one sweep of his paw. He jumped clear of the bear, pulled his knife and yelled to me: "Give it to him!" I poked the gun up close to his ear and blowed him through. The old man looked at me, and said: "Well done, Bud. The courage of a boy has saved my life." It was sweet music to me.

Muskrat were also great sport and quite profitable. We trapped them in the river bog [marshes and swamp land where the water was shallow]. We ran from one to two hundred traps every night and always caught about 25 to 50 rats. Their skins sold for ten cents apiece. Otter skins sold for a dollar a foot, and with the fish we caught and bear meat for food, we lived comfortable in the wilderness. High cost of living and hard times? There were no such things.

In the winter, when snow was four feet deep on the level and temperatures 20 to 40 below zero, we hunted moose and deer. On snowshoes and with a little crust of snow to hold up the dogs, we would seek out the yards where the deer wintered. These yards were made by deer congregating in a mass, constantly moving and treading the snow down to the earth, leaving them a clear place in which to stay, with snow four to seven feet deep forming a wall around them. Actually these yards were death traps for the deer when man chanced upon them. We would force the deer out into the deep snow with the dogs, where they became bogged down, then slay them at will. We killed only for meat, never for the mere sport of it. Game was our food.

Every winter Father made a trip with the team to Montreal, eighty miles, for supplies and to sell our furs, no matter how deep the snow or how cold the weather. He was a powerful man and a great wrestler, collar and elbow, and could hop and kick seven-and-a-half feet high—that is, standing on one foot, kick with the other and light on the foot he was standing on, and all done by the strength of one leg. He was champion of Stanstead County and held the belt.

For my brothers and me, one of our great sports in winter was racing down the long, steep hills on our Indian sleds when a little crust had formed on the snow. We would jump drifts on the hills at high speed and fly a hundred feet through the air before landing. I remember once hitting a big pine dead center, splitting my sled in two, leaving me sitting astraddle of the tree with the breath knocked out of me. I was badly stove up for a long time. I look back now and marvel why we were not killed by some of the stunts we used to perform while flying down those hills like greased lightning.

CHAPTER II

Out of the Woods into the Village

In 1852, another uncle of mine who had just returned from the California gold fields bought Father's farm, and we moved to the village. Consequently, a busier world was opened to me.

Father bought a house in Magog at the foot of Magog Lake and erected a large sawmill on the river at the head of the rapids. He associated himself with a lumberman named Ralph Merry and was actively engaged in this enterprise the next several years. He read a great deal and did his own thinking. He had strong convictions and the manliness and courage to proclaim and advocate them forcibly and convincingly. He took a very active part in municipal affairs and was looked upon as one of the most pronounced opponents of the liquor license system and consistent supporter of prohibition. Despite these beliefs, he was much appreciated by everyone, boozer and teetotaler alike. He was soon elected Mayor of Magog and a member of the County Council and Warden of the County. Later, he became Justice of the Peace and Clerk of the Common Court and Captain in the 3rd Battalion of Stanstead Militia under His Excellency Sir Edmund Walker Head, Baronet and Governor General of British North America.

He became interested in spirit phenomena, though little was known about it then. He used to hold circles in the house to investigate spirit manifestations and determine for himself whether there was anything to it. Mother's brother, Benjamin Sampson, who owned ship yards at Medford, Massachusetts, six miles from Boston, was a spiritualist, and he brought his wife and my half sister, Ellen, to Canada for a visit. This being the first time I had seen Ellen, we had to be introduced as brother and sister. It was her first time out of the city, but she seemed to realize what liberty meant. She was like a wild duck and made a great mate for me.

Uncle Ben was also a hypnotist and did many wonderful things with his wife. A fellow in the village made a great blow that no one could mesmerize him. One morning Ben happened to meet him on the street. It was raining hard. He caught him at a glance and made the fellow follow him and would keep asking him why he was following. But he kept at Uncle Ben's heels like a little dog. Finally Ben told him to walk in the gutter, that it would do him good. He obeyed at once, and got good and wet, and a big crowd gathered to see the fun. Then Ben made a few passes and brought him out, telling him never to brag again that no one could hypnotize him for he was an easy subject. After that the fellow always crossed the street when he saw Ben coming.

Spirit phenomena, Ben explained, was a different thing entirely. He held circles at our house for demonstration before he left. One night as he was cautioning the spirits not to be too rough for they might break the table, a man named Newton got excited and cried out, "Smash it, I will pay for it!" No quicker said than the table went into the air and came down with a crash, splintering off the legs. This so interested Newton that he followed my Uncle to Boston. He came back convinced that spirit return was a fact and swore that he had talked to his dead wife.

Father never was quite satisfied. He always asked, no matter how conclusive the evidence, "How do I know but what something within me, or all of us, does this thing?" He remained an agnostic. As for myself, I didn't care whether it was true or not so long as I had fun during those spooky interludes.

I kept hunting and trapping with my grandfather and enjoying my wild nature, and became quite a wrestler and athlete for a boy my age. I had to go back to school but, as before, books were the bane of my existence. I continued to get lickings at both ends of the line—at school and when I got home.

Finally I ran away and went to work in some mills near Magog splintering logs for broom sticks on a buzz saw. But the first time I ripped my hand on the saw, I quit the broom stick job and went home to Mother. Mother gave me her sympathy, Father gave me a licking, and all was forgiven and forgotten—until I was sent back to school.

Reading, writing and arithmetic was just too much for me. This time I ran off and got a job in a woolen factory, determined to stick it out and make my own way. Father was just as determined that I should stay home. He wasn't long finding me. On our way back he cut some birch rods. He had made up his mind to put an end to this runaway business, and I thought he was going to put an end to my business. He made an impression that lasted several days. But I simply could not sit still in school.

Through Mother, I finally coaxed Father into letting me change to the lumber business. He put me to hauling logs to the mill with sledge and a yoke of oxen. It was five miles to the mill through deep snow and heavy timber. But they became the happiest five miles of my life. There were no books to disturb the pleasure of living. I was reading the great book of all knowledge—nature. And I read her through and through. It was hard work, and a man's job. But it agreed with me.

When a bob sledge ran over me and banged me up considerable, I didn't complain. Another time, while felling a tree, I cut my foot open with an ax and limped home two miles, leaving a trail of blood. Mother wanted Father to fetch a doctor, but he said it wasn't necessary. "I'll sew up the cut," he told her. "Get a needle and thread."

Mother refused and started for the doctor. Father got the necessary items, and holding me down so I could not jump about, he took my leg between his thighs and commenced sewing away like darning a potato sack. I yelped and yelled, but he didn't stop until he had finished.

That foot laid me up a long time, but I suffered more from a lack of something to do. One day while alone I got out Father's violin and begin to pick out some of his old tunes. By noon I was playing Fisher's Hornpipe and the Soldier's Joy. When Mother came home and found me fiddling like an old timer, she thought it would be fun to surprise Father. While he was at supper that evening, I began playing his old tunes in the other room. He dropped his knife and fork and looked about as if something had struck him on the head.

"Who's the devil laying on my fiddle?" he asked, gruffly.

Mother told him it was me. He wanted to know where I had learned to play. She told him I had picked it up on my own. He said nothing more, but when he had finished eating, he came in and asked for the fiddle. I handed it over quickly, sensing trouble. But it didn't come as expected. He quietly tuned the instrument and handed it back to me. "Now, play the Soldier's Joy," he told me.

I started, but that was as far as I got. With the fiddle in tune, I could not play the darned thing. I had learned the pieces with the instrument out of tune, and that was the only way I could play them. It sure took the conceit out of me, but it was the beginning of my musical career.

I learned to tune the old fiddle and began playing pieces as they should be. I learned to play several other musical instruments, from French Horn to accordian, and soon was very much in demand for dances and other gatherings.

As soon as I was back on both feet, however, my active disposition sought mischief. Father had a wild horse that he drove. Everybody was afraid of him. I decided, having been cooped up so long, to have some real fun in as unusual fashion as possible. I had been kicked by this very horse, and it was my desire to conquer him. With brother Warren's reluctant assistance, we hitched the wild boy to Father's buggy and proceeded to take a ride.

Everything went fine a couple of miles, until we came to a long hill. Not satisfied with his good behavior to this point, I laid on

14

the whip. If he wasn't going to show some action, I was going to make him. I wanted to see how fast he could go down that hill. I soon found out. With a snort and a kick, the horse took the bit and we fairly flew through the air. I tried to keep him in the road, but he was kicking and bucking every direction. Then a rein broke, and there was no controlling the movements of this whirlwind. We were helpless and there was nothing to do but hang on. This I did, whooping and yelling with all my might, while my brother was crying and attempting to jump out.

I saw nothing but fun in the escapade and began whipping the frisky steed all the more. That settled things in a hurry. He leaped the ditch at the side of the road, broke loose from the buggy and ran kicking and snorting across the field, leaving me in the ditch in a somewhat uncomfortable position. I crawled from under the wrecked buggy, turned a somersault to determine that I was not hurt much, and started looking for Warren. He was nowhere in sight. At dusk, I met him limping down the hill minus his hat and boots. He had jumped out unbeknownst to me and in landing had stove out his boot soles.

We arrived home after dark, looking as though we had been run through a threshing machine. Father demanded an explanation. I told him I didn't think one was necessary, that things spoke for themselves. But he assured me that one was in order, and proceeded to do all the explaining in his usual masterful manner, using a hickory stick for a gavel.

This was in 1854, one of the many years that had been set for the world to come to an end. Although I have forgotten the exact month, I shall never forget the day.

One of our neighbors named Peter Mittson had extreme confidence in the end of the world. With the other members of his family, he donned a white robe and climbed to the top of his house so he would be as close to heaven as possible when the dreadful moment arrived. He had sold and given away everything he owned, believing he would not need them after that day. He began praying aloud from the housetop, and exactly at 12 noon, he jumped off the roof to heaven. But someone had made a mistake, for he did not go up but came right down, with considerable speed and much to his surprise and disgust. He landed on the ground with such a dull thud that it knocked all the prayer out of Peter! It must have been a terrible disappointment for one so sincere in his belief. It knocked some horse sense into him, as you shall see.

He had deeded his farm to Father, who had no desire to keep the place when Peter awakened. To Father's surprise, he refused to take it back, priding himself on being a man of his word. That was all very well with father, but he finally persuaded Peter to take the money he offered him for the property. Peter and his family then moved further into the wilderness to begin life anew.

Another tragic thing happened that fateless day to a very beautiful sixteen-year-old girl named Amanda Young. Her father had preached to her so much about the world coming to an end that she went temporarily insane. She ran into the woods in great fear of this hellfire and brimstone picture that had been forced upon her mind. Nobody seemed able to find her. With the aid of an Indian friend, I found her trail. We came upon her sitting at the bank of a small stream, crying. She had always liked me, but I was afraid that the moment she saw us she would become frightened again and try to elude us. I instructed the Indian to go to the opposite side of the stream and approach her. When she saw the Indian, she screamed and fled in terror, running into my arms as I expected. She fought furiously until I made her understand who I was and managed to lead her home.

I could do more with her than her folks, and they persuaded me to take her to dances and parties in hopes of restoring her mind. This I did, much to my chagrin, for the poor girl fell in love with me. I succeeded in talking her out of that when she came to her senses a few months later. She never regained her health, and died a few years afterward.

I remember another peculiar fellow in those days named Steve Chapman, who lived about two miles from us near the lake. He had a great habit of taking things that didn't belong to him—

sort of a mania, as it seems to be with some folks today. However, I never knew him to take anything out of his reach. He lived in an old shack with most of the glass broken out of the windows. The holes were stuffed with rags to keep out the cold and rain. He had a young daughter, Sally, and a son two years older than me. When the wind would shift in the night, old Steve would yell out: "Sal, shift the rags." And up his daughter would get and change the rags from one side of the house to the other, for there were only enough rags to fill the holes on one side of the house at a time.

Steve wasn't exactly a fool, even though he was a thief and twice as lazy. He possessed a subtle humor that once in a while crept from his vacuum brain and found voice, to wit: One day while working in his field—a rare thing for Steve to be doing—he sent his son for a jug of water. The boy took his time. When he finally returned, Steve said to him: "Son, stand up beside your dad." You bet he did, right quick. And Steve said, "Why, son, how you have grown since you've been gone. You're almost as tall as I am." Then old Steve proceeded to instruct him in a lesson in haste with the tip of his boot.

The officers finally came after Steve for some small theft. They found him hiding high up in the flue of his stone fireplace and took him to the county lock-up. There was no door on the jail, and two guards were stationed at the entrance with their guns crossed. Crafty old Steve began walking back and forth, slowly and thoughtfully, apparently paying them no heed. He kept this up for hours until the guards got so use to this kind of perpetual motion they became lax in their duty. Working nearer the doorway, Steve suddenly bounded past them, dashed into a barn nearby and hid under some hay. The guards were unable to find him in the barn and passed through into the cow yard. Steve jumped out of the hay and ran into the woods.

Steve had no place to go, however, and that night he was captured. He was sentenced to prison at hard labor, which was pretty tough on Steve. He was put to dressing down a millstone. He worked slowly, doing a fine job, but after it had passed the inspection of his guards and they had complimented him on his work, he picked up a sledge and split it in two. So they placed him in a deep tank of water where he was forced to pump or drown. He would wait until the water began to strangle him, then pump like a demon, cursing the guards and their system of punishment. When he got out of the tank, he attempted another escape, and was shot to death.

There was another old fellow who ran a general store in the village the boys used to torment a great deal. His name was Abbott, but we called him "Pinch Copper." If he had not been so miserly and constantly cheating his customers in his weights, etc., we would have been more mild with him. As it was, everybody was seeking a chance to get even. We used to tie his wrapping twine to some boy and then yell, "Fire!" and all run out of the store. The boy with the twine would run faster than the rest and not stop until the whole ball of string unwound. He got the village officer after us, and for this he paid dearly.

Skunks were never a great source of torment for me. I had mastered the knack of handling them while trapping with my grandfather, so I was elected to visit vengeance upon Pinch Copper. He had just built a house, a swell affair in those days, with a knocker on the door, the first I had ever seen. The largest, most odoriferous animal I could find was attached tail foremost to the knob of the front door. To the knocker I fastened a string, stretching it across the street where I concealed myself with several other junior devils of the village in a clump of bushes. It was late at night and old Pinch had retired. A couple of pulls on the knocker brought him to the door in a Moses-like nightshirt. When he swung the door inward, he carried the squirming, perfumed squirter into the house. Someone inside yelled, "Phew!" I think it must have been Mrs. Pinch Copper, as her smellers were more acute than the old man's. A pull on another string gave the skunk his freedom.

The four-legged fellow was certainly more than excited. Through the open door and by the light inside, we saw him scampering over furniture and under chairs. The old man began yelling and jumping up and down like a whooping Indian. Then his wife appeared with a broom and attempted to "shoo!" our friend out the doorway. He wouldn't "shoo" a bit and became more excited than ever, simply saturating the room and its contents and two occupants in a manner most pleasing to see. At last the skunk spied the doorway and darted across the porch, heading directly for the bushes where we were hidden and polluting the sweet evening air. Old Pinch ran out on the porch and started yelling for the police. We lost no time making ourselves scarce. And well might we, for a no more diabolical trick was ever committed than what that skunk did to that house. Nobody was ever lion-hearted enough to live in it again. Finally it became a ghost-mansion, haunted by "speerits" and skunks, half-human, some did say.

The next morning every parent in the village went sniffing around their young'uns trying to detect if they had anything to do with old Pinch's downfall. But ne'er an odor did they find. To this day I am the unknown and unpunished criminal, though not proud of it, looking back now with something of a conscience.

There was no end to the number of tricks we played on pod Pinchy. I will record one more and then let him rest in peace.

One evening a big, burly fellow was lounging on the porch of Pinch Copper's store. For want of something to do, he was permitting the boys to strike him on his expanded chest as hard as they could to show how strong he was. Inside, old Pinch bent over the counter with his specks on the end of his nose doing some figuring. The big fellow was standing in front of a barrel of salt near the large glass window. I stepped up to him and asked to demonstrate my strength on his puffed out chest. He laughed, noting my small stature, which was very deceiving in the matter of strength and body quickness.

"Sure," he said insolently. "Fire away, little boy, before your ma comes along and takes you home."

The words had no sooner left his mouth than I acted. With arms bent and the tips of my elbows extended in front of me, I threw my whole weight into a sudden plunge that took him in the lower part of the chest just above the stomach. He doubled with a grunt of pain, lost his balance, staggered backward over the barrel of salt and crashed through the window, landing at Pinchy's feet. The lion in the specks roared and out he came with a big rawhide whip he used to chase us away, slashing and cutting at everything in sight. Long before he reached the porch we had scooted around the corner of the store, where we stood, whooping and yelling with glee. Unable to reach us with the whip, he re-entered the store and vented his rage on the big fellow, who was picking himself up in blank amazement. At the first slash of the rawhide, he landed one on Pinchy's jaw, laying him cold, then took after me down the road. I outran him easily.

The next day old Pinch swore out a warrant for my arrest for disturbing the peace as though there was never any peace around that neck of the woods where us boys roamed at will. My father, being judge of the court at the time, dismissed the case for lack of evidence. Pinch took exception, and while he had Father in a position where he had to appear pious, dignified and not act ungentlemanly by administering physical violence, said some pretty unkind things to him.

When court adjourned, Father went to old Pinch's store. The crowd followed, with us boys in the rear, as it was commonly agreed something of interest was about to happen.

Father walked up to Pinch, gave his nose a twist, and demanded an apology. Quaking with fear, Pinch whimpered to the crowd: "Take notice, gentlemen, he snubbed my nose."

Father said, "I did not snub your nose, Mr. Abbott. I simply pinched it—like this!" And he gave old Pinch's nose another twist. After he had backed him the length of the room and repeated this several times, Pinch got so excited he snatched up a loose board from the end of the counter and swung it at Father's head. Father merely met the board with his clenched right fist, splitting it down the center as though it had been cleaved with an ax.

He stood looking at the old miser with the terrible grin on his face I had seen so often. Things usually happened then in a fashion not easily forgotten. With bare fists, I had once seen him subdue

20

three lumberjacks armed with spikes and cudgels. He stood quivering from head to foot like an angry animal, but in the next instant he controlled himself. He turned and walked from the store, took me by the hand, and led me home without another word. I had escaped municipal punishment, only to receive a more strenuous and private one that evening in the woodshed where the honor and name of the family was habitually perpetuated.

I kept away from Pinch Copper's store after that and spent more time at the mill. Old Shippy, Father's boss sawyer, was a very close friend of mine. He was a large, strong fellow, always ready for a fight, and we had some great times together. Two reckless boys never worked around more dangerous machinery. Paring our fingernails on the teeth of the revolving saw was a common thing with us.

One day Shippy found a plug hat and was sporting it around the mill. We got in a scuffle, and I took him down and sawed the crown off the hat still on his head. Running and jumping over the five-foot circular saw revolving twelve thousand revolutions per minute was another of our playful stunts. When my dog had a litter of pups, Shippy sawed off their tails to give them a high-toned air. This beat cutting them off with a hatchet. It was quick and completely painless.

Once Shippy caught my dog by the tail and threw her into the mill pond. I went for him to throw him in too. As he struggled to the slip door, he pulled my coat over my head, blinding me. We were ten feet above the water and logs, and in order to force him through the door, I threw myself out, taking him headfirst with me. He broke loose and landed on the logs; I went between them to the bottom of the pond, smothered in my coat. I kept my presence of mind and swam on the bottom until I struck the flume rack, crawled to the top and out with my coat still over my head. Shippy was ready to dive after me when I made my appearance. I had been under a good five minutes.

I now put in the winter at the great mountain lumber camp at Oxford as sawyer. My job was to follow the choppers and cut the trees into logs of different lengths. Our camp living was potatoes, turnips, good old pork and beans, Johnny cake and maple molasses, fish and wild game. No room for doctors in a camp like that. Our amusements were snowshoe racing, wrestling, and dancing, with plenty of pumpkin pie and good rum to wash it down. One night we were invited to the village to take part in a fancy ball. Fur cap, red shirt, pants, and boots constituted our wardrobe, and you can bet we walked into the ballroom on time. We drew no curiosity, we were in style, as they call it now. One of the boys got a little too much Tom and Jerry, and a smart alec stole his fancy belt, like all of us wore around our waists. To get even, we found his team and cut the line from the harness, which made several good belts for the leather was wide and new.

The real fun came in the spring. The snow melted, the river opened, and the log rolling and driving began. We rolled into the water the logs that we had hauled and piled on the banks during the winter, then ran them loose down the river. Using set-poles, handpikes, and spikes on the soles of our boots, we rode them to civilization, taking about two months for the trip.

Speaking of health, strength and endurance! You slept on the river banks on frozen ground in wet clothes, got up at daybreak with your pants frozen stiff, thawed out by the fire, and back to the logs again. Two skilled positions had to be filled— braking and bringing up the rear. This was my work. I could ride any log that would hold me and float.

The first week out one of the owners came out on the logs, and to make things interesting, I decided to give him a bath. I waited until we were in an opening, then leaped to the side of his log and gave it a quick turn, throwing him into the water. He had boasted about being on a ship, and I thought he could swim. But he didn't know enough to go to the end of the log and pull himself out. He kept trying to climb upon the side like a dog, only to be rolled under every time. The poor fellow was about gone when I pulled back and rescued him.

When we reached the lake, we boomed the logs and crossed with the wind, then broke the boom to let them all go loose down the mouth of the river. At that time we had the biggest jam at the head of the rapids ever known, and nobody dared go down under that mountain of timber and hunt the key log and break the gain. Shippy and I agreed to try it.

People lined the banks to witness the dangerous feat. The logs had blocked and joined under the dam below and piled twenty feet high. We knew that every join had a key log, which was the first thing to find, at the bottom as a rule. Equipped with hand-pikes, we looked out a safe route to the bottom and began to explore cautiously. I soon discovered the key log. The anxiety of the people above was as great as the roar of the water. My father had arrived and was yelling at us to come out before we were killed.

I told Shippy to look out a safe route for our escape, and I would follow. When he gave the signal, I threw out the log with one swing and a hideous yell, dropped my handpike and took after him. The tangled mountain of timber came crashing and grinding downward. But we had a faster start and Shippy's judgment was good. He made his jumps sure with great speed, and I close at his heels. We reached the top and safety amidst great cheering, and the mass of logs disappeared swiftly into the rapids below where the crowd had expected us to go.

Poor Shippy met his fate a short time afterward. He slipped on a log and fell in front of the saw and both his legs were amputated above the knees. He was alone at the mill, and before help arrived, he bled to death.

CHAPTER III

My First Trip to the United States—
Unshipped and Foiled in My Plan to Work
Passage Around Cape Horn to California,
I Return to Canada—Back to the States—
I Miss Two Golden Opportunities in
Pennsylvania

After Shippy's accident, I became uneasy and dissatisfied, and took up trapping and hunting again with my old grandfather among the Indians. Since my first trip in the forest, the Indians had liked me. I let my hair grow long and began to dress in their manner—in buckskin attire. I spent all my spare time with them, and was so full of tricks they called me "white man-devil."

I believe my brother Albert was the first to call me Joe. It remains a mystery to me where he got the name, for my father and mother always called me by my Christian name—Ed, for short. When I returned to the village from my trips in the woods, I wore my long hair and Indian dress, and everybody started calling me "Buckskin Joe." That title has stuck with me ever since.

The next spring, while in from a big hunting expedition, I went with Albert sixteen miles to Sherbrooke to see Howe's Circus. There were seats and a place called "the Pit" where you could stand up for a quarter. We went to the Pit. Several hunters and lumbermen there knew me and pushed me into the ring to act up a little. I did a couple of ditties, turned a few flips and somersaults, and ran back. They began shouting, and in the excitement, I crawled through and up on the seats where I could see. Some circus fellows spotted me, and up they came to put me back in the

Pit, but those husky hunters and lumbermen sang out, "Let him alone, or down comes the shanty!"

The circus fellows squared off, but before trouble could start, the head clown stepped up and announced that any boy who could do what I had done in the ring was entitled to a free pass to the show. Three cheers went up and I held the fort.

When the show was over, the old clown came to me and took me back to his dressing room. He asked if I wanted to go with the show and learn the business.

"You bet," I said.

He asked whose boy I was, and I told him I was an orphan. So he took me to the hotel and introduced me to the rest of the show people as his boy. I was having a good time, when all at once Albert showed up and spoiled everything.

I told the old clown I would have to leave, that the stage was all set for Magog. We never saw each other again, but my circus aspiration had been aroused once more.

I constantly practiced all the tricks I had learned. I could turn somersaults backwards in the street with my overcoat on, and frequently while dancing would turn a row of flip-flaps down the center to the bottom of the line. There was not much etiquette in this, but the novelty made up for its lack. It was great sport for the crowd, as well as myself, and my nature to outdo others.

That summer I was engaged to go with the Joe Lentland Circus of New York. Father objected, and I was disappointed once more.

About this time the famous phrenologist, Professor Nichols, came along. Father, who believed some in it, invited him to our home to examine my head and see what he could find. I told him there sure was something in my head and he didn't have to use a fine-toothed comb. As soon as the professor placed his hands on me he looked at Father, and said, "You can cluck like an old hen to her chickens but it will do no good. This chap is looking for a wider world and is bound to have room to spread. He must travel and see for himself. He will not stay among these hills. But never fear, for he can take care of himself. Let him go."

That night at supper I noticed Father looked and acted a little differently. At last he spoke, and said, "Young man, when are you going to leave us?"

I felt kind of funny. I guessed at what was coming, so I made a stand and told him I was planning to run away with another boy my age through the great wilderness to the city of Montreal.

His grave remark was, "Remember, son, my door is always open, and always will be to my children to go and come whenever they please."

That sobered me. The wind went out of my sails and the romance of the journey departed in a minute. I didn't feel like running away now that I had leave to go. I had nothing to run away for. He had hit me below the belt, and it was the hardest blow he ever dealt me.

It was Mother again who compromised the situation. She wanted to visit her folks in Boston, and as I wished to see a city and experience a change of scenery, we arranged with Father for the money and took the stage for a hundred mile trip to connect with the Vermont railroad. We arrived six miles from Medford, Massachusetts, where my uncles, aunts and half-sister lived (Uncle Ben had become overseer in the Charleston Navy Yards), and I celebrated the 4th of July, Mother's birthday, in the United States. I was out two days and a night without sleep with one of my cousins, Dennis Fullor. He drove a truck wagon in South Boston and knew the city like a book. I reckon we saw all of it and I told myself, *if this is what they call civilization, I believe I am going to like the change.*

I went down to the Navy Yards with Uncle Ben and boarded a ship, a cruiser about to sail on a six-month voyage. It looked so inviting I thought I would like to live on it. The Captain came around and said to me, "Whose boy are you?"

"Oh," said I, "anybody's boy."

"How would you like to sail with me on this ship?"

I told him it would suit me just fine.

He said, "We will be off in the morning, and I have a sailor suit made for you. Here is a cap and jacket. Put them on."

They sure fit good, and I thought I was strictly in, but Uncle

27

Ben happened to spy me while he was inspecting the ship. He very quickly unshipped me and gave the Captain the very devil and took me back to Medford for the folks to see all togged up. Mother wanted to know where I thought I was going. I told her I thought it a good chance to get a free ride to California where I could get rich digging gold. She thought we had better return home, but before time came to go, I fixed it with her for me to stay and work with my cousin in the city.

I went over in South Boston and boarded with Dennis Fullor. We decided to go to California, as he had a brother there in the gold fields, and made arrangements to work our passage around Cape Horn. Upon reconsidering the matter, we decided to write his brother to send us the money and avoid the hardships and danger. We waited, but the money did not come. I told him I would strike out into the country to the north and get work and help raise the money. He would let me know as soon as he heard from his brother and I would be ready. I started north, but no work and no word from Fullor, and I finally drifted home to Canada. That ended our scheme.

Since I had been on a big trip to civilization, everybody except old Pinchy was glad to see me. A big squirrel-hunting contest was ready to start—Hattly against Magog, in a three-day hunt. The side that brought in the most squirrel heads was to get their supper, dance, and entertainment at the loser's expense. Our side won, and the first thing to come off was the championship wrestling for that country.

They picked me to take the ring for Magog. Hattly had two champions to put against me. Their manager, Sam Turner, who knew me, warned them that I was a hard one. The ring formed and the betting commenced. Time came to enter the ring, and I jumped in at once. Hattly champion Number 1 came in leisurely— a tall, well-built man, but too cocky to please me. He looked me over and remarked, "I expected to wrestle a man, not a boy."

A cry went up from my side, "Two to one the boy throws you!" He put up all the money he had and so did his backers. Then we jumped to the center. I reached for his collar and elbow, and he laid onto mine. I asked, "Are you ready?"

He replied, quite unconcerned, "Oh, anytime." He hadn't got the "anytime" out of his mouth when I knocked both feet from under him, and he lay sprawled on his back.

A big yell went up, and his manager said, "I told you not to take chances." He leaped to his feet, fighting mad, and swore he could lick me. I turned a quick somersault and was ready to light into him when the referees jumped in and caught us. They announced him out and called for the other man.

Champion Number 2 entered the ring, and a Hattly cheer went up. His name was Hines—a man my size and a perfect gentleman. The chill that seizes a man who excels in this sport was upon me; I knew I had something to do. Time was called and we stepped into position for square-hold wrestling. I asked if he was ready, and he announced that he was. Science was now displayed and many feelers thrown out. A sparing with the feet began. It was soon evident to the crowd that we were well matched and all would be very interesting, for neither of us could lay the other on his back. He was like the Irishman's flea—when I thought I had him, I had him not. He could say the same for me.

After an hour of this, and using all the strength and skill we possessed, the crowd begin to sympathize and advise us to call it a draw. "No," I said. I knew now it was a matter of endurance, which it proved to be, for he grew so weak I got him off balance and followed through until he fell with me on top. The announcement was made, "Time—two hours. Fair fall. Championship to Magog."

We were wrapped in blankets and taken to the hotel. It was called the greatest match ever pulled off in that country, and you should have seen my father and old Tim Rexford of Hattly— those old champions standing around shivering like men with the ague. I think it was the first thing I ever did for which Father expressed enjoyment and appreciation. He gave a big supper and a blow-out ball.

My grandfather had the greatest time of all, and to celebrate the occasion, we took off for the wilderness and spent all winter trapping and hunting with the Indians. When we returned in the spring of 1859, Grandfather decided to change his hunting grounds and go west among the Sioux in Minnesota, and I decided to have another look at civilization.

I left Magog on May 10, taking the stage sixteen miles to the railroad where I bought a ticket to Westfield, New York. From there I went to visit my Uncles Ralph and Mose Hoyt, who lived near Panama, eighteen miles from Westfield. I arrived in the evening, surprising them all, and had a jolly time with relatives and friends named Spinney and Webster who also had moved to this country from my native land. The girls and myself had grown so we did not know each other. The Spinneys and Websters owned farms on what was known as Town Line, five miles out. I took out my fiddle, and the fun commenced. To be sure I played to please the girls.

The most remarkable thing I remember was fiddling their dog to death. He got to howling, which put all hands to laughing and shouting, and I kept right on fiddling until he took a fit and died on the spot. We postponed long enough to bury the animal, then went on with my dog-killing music.

It got noised around that a new fiddler had hit the country and that he was a hummer. I cut my hair and spruced up to please everybody, and was soon invited to Jamestown. I was introduced to Professor Lyons, who had been engaged to furnish the music for a big ball to take place at Busta Eye Corners on 4th of July night. After hearing a few pieces, he thought it remarkable that I could play like that and know nothing about music.

"My second violinist is sick," he said. "Will you take his place?"

"Why," said I, "I wouldn't know a note from a bull's foot."

"They will never know the difference," said he, "and I have to furnish six instruments."

"In that case," said I, "I will try, but play in easy keys."

I accompanied him to the hall and he introduced me as a new violinist from Buffalo—one of Tom Cook's pupils. He had some quite large-sized books to play from and, of course, the second violin book was placed in front of me. It was new and very attractive. The crowd formed for the dance and the band commenced to play. You can bet I was playing too. I bore down hard when I knew I was right. When they turned a leaf, I turned one also.

Someone in the crowd said, "Ain't he just fine?" And another, "He is from Buffalo—one of Tom Cook's pupils."

A young lady shied up to Lyons and whispered, "He can beat your old player all to death."

"Oh, yes." Mr. Lyons replied, "he can play my music with his eyes shut. He is a wonder. "

"Oh do, Professor, give me an introduction."

"Sure, I will," and turning to me, he said, "Professor Hoyt, allow me to introduce to you an accomplished musician, Miss Florence Lord." And I thought to myself, *Oh God!*

"I am pleased to meet you, Miss Lord, and hope for further acquaintance."

Now I faked it all right and made a big hit. It was more fun than trapping and hunting with my grandfather, and the Professor said he never had a more enjoyable evening in his life. He gave me two dollars and promised to give me lessons at half price. So I got a job in Hazelton's Woolen Factory running a set of cards, boarded with the family, and on July 18, began taking lessons on the violin. I played with the orchestra regularly, took up the clarinet and cornet, and joined the Brass Band of the fire company.

There was one fellow in the fire company who claimed to be a great athlete. Thinking to gain a point for himself, he challenged me to a boxing match. I put on the gloves, but soon discovered he was too scientific for me. So I lit into him, hammer and tong, main strength and awkwardness, and so confused him that I knocked him onto a hot stove. He shouted, "Enough!" and I pulled him off to keep him from burning to death.

He asked, "Do you call that boxing?"

"Call it what you like," said I, "but you sure got the hot end of it." The boys nearly died laughing, and it sure took the conceit out of him.

It spread over town that I was also a good wrestler, and a match was made over in another mill. I appeared on the scene and was introduced to the crowd. The ring formed and time was called. I stepped to the center and laid hold of my man. Without asking if I was ready, and entirely unexpected, he threw me flat of my back. Some cheered—the majority knew it was unfair. I said, "I see that you have a new custom, but I am now onto your rules. Will you take hold again?"

He did, and I threw him as quickly as he had me. I said, "Now, take hold once more, for it is two best out of three."

"We will call it a draw," said he.

"Oh, no," said I. "I came to miss or lose. Neither of us has done any wrestling yet, so let us be decent about it. This fall will settle it."

The crowd insisted, so he walked to the center. We took hold and commenced sparing with our feet. He tried the hip lock, the grapevine, the trip and twitch, and the cross-to on me, and failed to make any work. But I had discovered his weak point. I watched my chance and caught him on a cross-to and threw him quickly and very hard on his back, and a yell went up for me.

I gained many friends in the town. I was promoted to spinner at the factory, and continued to take music lessons at night. Then, in August, I heard that Colonel Edwin L. Drake had brought in the first oil well on his land near Titusville, Pennsylvania.

[Up to this time the shale oil industry had made considerable progress in the United States. By distillation, a rich paraffin oil was extracted from the bituminous coal shales, and from this was manufactured a fair grade of illuminating oil called "kerosene." By 1859, nearly sixty establishments were engaged in its manufacture. The market for oil was limited, but Mr. Hoyt knew its value. The discovery of crude petroleum in commercial quantities would render the laborious process of obtaining a crude distillate from the shale rock no longer necessary.]

I obtained some lease forms and started forty miles south on foot with the idea of securing leases on all lands adjoining the discovery, but had the misfortune of meeting a couple of liars.

I met these fellows in the hills, and they discouraged me by saying that it was all a mistake—they had just come from Drake's land and he had struck nothing but artesian water.

I turned back and right there missed my golden opportunity. [On August 28, Drake's well began producing at a depth of 69½ feet. The oil rose to within ten feet of the surface. When equipped for pumping, it produced forty barrels a day, and the product sold readily at fifty cents a gallon or twenty dollars a barrel. As the news spread over the country, another well was completed near Rouseville, farther down Oil Creek. Hundreds of others were then started in the Oil Creek valley and up and down the Alleghenny River, and the rush to engage in the new industry was comparable to the excitement that followed the discovery of gold in California in 1848. Immediately the shale refineries adapted their works to the manufacture of illuminating oil from the crude product they secured from the Pennsylvania regions, and the petroleum industry was born.] Had I carried out my plan, I could have been Coal Oil Johnny, for it was this that made him. But if it had made as big a fool of me as it did him, I am the lucky one at last.

Instead of returning to Jamestown, I went back to Panama. Uncle Ralph Hoyt had discovered good indications of oil four miles from town. He organized a company to sink on the prospect and appointed me superintendent. A hundred feet down we lost our drill. I invented an instrument to get it out of the hole and went on with the work, but am sorry to say we never struck oil. With our crude methods we could not go deep enough.

I took a job with the railroad, worked in a pail factory for a while, then went back to fiddling. I had become pretty well known over the country and could play in all sixteen instruments. Finally I organized a little show for the road. I had a nigger named Abe who swallowed a saucer full of pebbles every night. He was a good dancer and banjo player, and together, we gave a good entertainment.

We went over in Pennsylvania to the lumber camps and the Indian reservation, then put into the Alleghenny on a log raft and went down to Pittsburgh and Alleghenny City. We were stopped at Pittsburgh. The Secessionists had fired on Fort Sumter and all was excitement.

I disbanded the show and took up lodging in Alleghenny City. While there I made the acquaintance of a pretty young widow with two children, very wealthy and the owner of a brick city block. She promised me an easy time the rest of my days if I would marry her, and I missed the second golden opportunity of my life. I told her no—there was too much war in the air already.

CHAPTER IV

On the Warpath—My First Year in the Civil War

[The years of bitter controversy between the North and the South over the slavery question flared into war in the spring of 1861. The newly elected President, Abraham Lincoln, in his speeches en route to Washington and in his inaugural address on March 4, declared his opposition to any interference with slavery in the states where it existed, and conferences were held by leading statesmen and politicians of different sections in an attempt to avert the crisis. But the efforts were in vain. The South established a secession government styled the Confederate States of America with Jefferson Davis as president and, as an initial step in a startling program to seize United States customhouses, arsenals, forts, and other public property within their borders, attacked Fort Sumter, in Charleston harbor, South Carolina. Fort Sumter fell on April 14, 1861, and immediately Lincoln issued a call for 75,000 three-months' volunteers. The North and West responded with such enthusiasm and determination that if sufficient arms and accoutrements had been available, there would have been enough men in the field to have scattered and destroyed the insurgent army in three months. Instead, official inaction enabled the Confederates to make a fearless assault upon Union soldiers while passing through Baltimore, destroy vital railroads and telegraphs, seize the Norfolk navy yard, and advance within sight of Washington itself. There were 10,000 troops within a day's march of the Potomac who, any night, might have taken Arlington Heights and held its crowded camps at their mercy. Not until May 24 did a force of 15,000 Union soldiers cross the Potomac, throw up a line of strong earthworks, and mount guns sufficient to insure the safety of the city. This passive resistance, with the time of the regiments enlisted under the three-months' call fast passing, accomplished nothing. The enemy had only to wait behind their entrenchments, then attack without meeting more than nominal resistance, as reflected in Mr. Hoyt's biography.]

I enlisted in a Pennsylvania regiment at Pittsburgh in May, 1861. We were ready for action, but it was weeks before we were en route to the first big battle that took place July 21 at Bull Run, or Bloody Run, Virginia. This appeared to be a free-for-all fight. We were under General Patterson, who was supposed to cut Johnston off and never did. [General Patterson, with some 20,000 Union troops—mostly Pennsylvania militia—was at Chambersburg, Pennsylvania. General Joseph E. Johnston, with an equal number of Confederates, was at Harper's Ferry, on the Potomac, watching him. On July 7 Patterson advanced from Chambersburg to Hagerstown, Maryland. Johnston evacuated Harper's Ferry and retreated upon Winchester, Virginia. Patterson crossed the Potomac, and after trifling away a week's time, got within nine miles of Johnston's army by July 15. Instead of attacking, or attempting to get between Winchester and the Shenandoah River, as he had orders to do, Patterson took his forces to Charleston, allowing the enemy to escape and form a junction via Manassas Gap which proved essential to Rebel success.] This move made me think him a traitor to the cause. If he had obeyed orders, Bull Run would have been a victory for the Union.

This being the end of our three-months' enlistment, we were sent to Erie, Pennsylvania, and disbanded. I was glad to get out anyway, for they had been slow to give us firearms and our grub was poor. We were eating old sea biscuits filled with maggots branded "B.C." No one seemed to know what those letters stood for until I solved the mystery. I told them they meant Before Christ—that was when they were made. The adjutant-general inspected us and we covered our flag staff with mottos to fit the occasion. I fixed up a guard with a wooden gun and placed him on duty walking around the pole with a sign on his back: "We are tough cusses, but can't eat hay."

After I was mustered out at Erie, I went to Panama, New York, to visit Uncle Ralph. My grandfather was there and tried to talk me into returning to Canada. I said, "No," that I was still on the warpath. In a few days I started back to Erie for my discharge papers, covering the distance of forty miles in eight hours on foot. My officers seemed glad to see me. They supposed I would re-enlist and appointed me Recruiting Sergeant, but after going to the adjutant's office and getting my pass so I could ride free on the railroad, I took the train to Jamestown and back to Panama, where I made arrangements with Captain Drake to recruit for the 49th New York State Volunteers, Colonel D. D. Bidwell, Commanding, City of Buffalo.

[The loss at Bull Run had stunned the North temporarily. Congress realized for the first time the danger which threatened the nation. Within thirty-three days it legalized acts and orders of the President; voted ten million dollars for purchase of arms locally and abroad; added eleven regiments to the regular army; raised the pay of the soldier to thirteen dollars a month, with a bounty of one hundred acres at the close of the war; undertook to indemnify the states for all expenses they might incur in raising, paying, subsisting, and transporting troops; and authorized the enlistment of a half-million volunteers.]

I was able to recruit a good many in Chautauqua County, New York. On August 26, 1861, I rounded them up in Panama, hired teams, and drove eighteen miles to meet Captain Drake at Westfield. It was a sad parting. I was presented with a flag and saber that had been used in the Revolutionary War. I made a farewell speech and the cheers went up as we drove off with our flag flying and dear ones sobbing and crying. Most of those boys never returned. As Sherman said, "War is hell."

37

We arrived in Westfield at night and went into camp. They wanted to elect me Lieutenant, which I refused. I was appointed Second Sergeant and acting Drill Sergeant for Company G, and we took the train from there to Buffalo and joined our regiment at Camp Porter. On August 30, we were mustered into federal service. Our regiment was now complete. On September 15, we drew our equipment, and on the 16th, received marching orders, packed, and took a special train for Washington, 1000 strong.

While marching to the train through the streets of Buffalo, I saw my grandfather for the last time. I broke ranks and crossed the street to greet him. He was on his way back to Canada, for his pet and favorite had left him. I tore a piece of braid and button from my uniform and told him to give it to Mother and tell her I would be home after the war and not to cry—that I would write often and was never born to be shot.

I have always felt it was my absence that caused him to be drowned in the Magog River in 1862. He had taken on a new man to run the lower rapids, and the boat upset. The old man grabbed the limb of a tree projecting out over the water, and there he hung. His companion drifted ashore and ran half a mile up the river to our mill and gave the alarm. My oldest brother jumped into a boat and shot over the dam and down to the tree ahead of them all, but Grandfather was not there. They found him two hours later across the river in the bottom of still water.

We boarded the train and arrived in New York City at 6 A.M. on the 18th and took quarters in the Park Barracks. It was so crowded we had to stand up all day, for the 43rd New York was there also. On the 21st we again boarded the train for Washington. At 3 o'clock the morning of the 22nd, we arrived in Philadelphia, took breakfast at the Soldiers' Relief, and at 3 P.M. arrived in Baltimore.

Here we had to march through the city two miles to the depot. The people looked very cross. One of our boys bought a piece of pie from an old lady that was poisoned and died from the effects. We captured the old woman, and with a guard of six, compelled her to lead us to the party who, she claimed, had forced her to sell pies to Union soldiers. She took us to an old house on a hill. The man didn't see us until we walked in. The old lady said, "That's him." We left him hanging on his own door.

At 8 P.M. we reached Washington. We took supper and laid on our guns all night. We were expecting an attack on the city at any time. [General George B. McClellan of the Ohio militia volunteers, a graduate of West Point and veteran of the Mexican War, commanded the Army of the Potomac. He had appointed his general staff, formulated his plans of organization, and laid out a system of fortifications across the river from Arlington to Alexandria. As fast as the new regiments arrived, they were formed into provisional brigades and assigned to camps for instruction and discipline.] On September 26, a heavy cannonading began in the direction of the heights, and by 1 P.M., we had our marching orders.

We packed and started for Virginia. No more train rides and good grub now. We crossed the Potomac over the Chain Bridge in the rain and mud to the scene of action. Night overtook us and we got separated in the brush and hills. We laid out all night, very tired and expecting the enemy. I told the boys it was a good initiation for what was to come. In the morning, we got together and made camp on a hill, called Camp Advance, and pitched our tents at a new fort we built called Ethan Allen, and another called Fort Smith.

We worked hard on the forts day and night, for the enemy's guns were in reaching distance, and every time the long roll sounded we would double quick into our forts for protection. We thought this was getting action in a hurry. On the 29th, we had hard fighting on our picket lines, and the next day we buried our dead at the fort. It begin to look like war.

[By the end of September, McClellan was able to report to the Secretary of War an aggregate strength of 168,318 men. Excepting those manning the defenses along the Potomac, there were 76,285 ready for active service in the field, with an artillery force of 228 guns. Despite constant pressure from the public and the press, the President, and the heads of departments in Washington, McClellan refused to move and spent another five months in preparation. His placidity is reflected in the diary which Mr. Hoyt kept during this build-up for the Peninsular Campaign of 1862.]

October 1st: In camp. Drilled our men and noncommissioned officers till 2 o'clock. All quiet.

2nd: Very warm. We drilled in the morning. Heavy cannonading in the direction of the Rebels. Worked on the fort in the afternoon. All worked hard.

3rd: Worked hard on the fort, the only thing we depend on.

4th: Had battalion drill in the afternoon. No rebels to be seen. The balloon went up and broke loose and went to Baltimore and came down—all safe and sound. A rather narrow escape for Professor Gow.

5th: I was on Sergeant of the Guard and our Regt. was going on picket, and I hired a sergeant to take my place so I could go. Eve—On duty at guard tent.

6th: Sunday. At three o'clock in the morning we all got ready and went on picket about four miles. I was put in the far advance post, the most dangerous one. I lay out all night waiting but no Rebels came. How I would like to shoot one.

7th: We were relieved at five in the morning and no one has been killed. We went back to camp, all very sleepy. Eve—Rained very hard.

8th: Great excitement. We are firing our guns out of the fort to try them. Eve—Go to bed, expecting a fight.

9th: Heavy firing off to the south. We think our pickets are attacked. We are all ready. Eve—We were ordered into the fort. We expect an attack, but all is quiet.

10th: We go back to our tents. I feel very lame. I took cold in the fort. All is quiet.

11th: I tried to drill but I am so lame I cannot. Eve—We had orders to march but they were countermanded and we lay in our tents.

12th: We had orders to march at seven. We marched to the

far advance post, 5 miles. Our cavalry killed two. We expected a fight. Eve—On our arms, expecting a fight.

13th: Sunday. All go to work clearing off a camp ground with our guns stacked. Some fighting on picket lines. Worked hard.

14th: Worked clearing off camp ground. Some killed on picket line.

15th: The ambulance came in with the wounded. Blood running out of the hind end in a stream.

16th: The long roll beat at two and we were in line of battle in five minutes. We stood there till morning and then went to our quarters. . . .

[The remainder of October was quiet. Hoyt spent most of his time on picket, at drill, dress parade, and inspection. "I also learned to tattoo," he noted. On October 26 the brigade "had a grand review by Major-Generals Smith and Hancock. Very bad music. We are now in Smith's Division." On October 31, "we were drawn up in line and inspected and mustered in for pay by Col. Taylor, acting. . . . Amount paid me—$35.13." Hoyt struck an acquaintance with a "Charles Wentworth and some of the Erie boys . . . went into the woods, built a fire, and played bluff (poker) till 11 P.M. Some XX came and we went on skirmish. . . ."]

November 3rd: I went over with a lieutenant and a squad to headquarters to guard some secessionist prisoners. 20,000 troops crossed the Potomac into Virginia today. We expect to fight soon.

[A fight failed to materialize, however. Rain and cold, blustery weather set in. "I tattooed a globe and the date of my enlistment on my legs and a little on my arm, played bluff in the woods, and had some fun."]

20th: Army of the Potomac is reviewed by General McClellan. A hundred and seventy thousand were reviewed. . . .

[By the end of November, heavy cannonading had begun from the south.]

December 1st: Sunday. A good deal of talk but little cider. Eve—Detailed 60 men for picket.

41

2nd: Up at three and my men ready for picket. I did not go. I feel sick. Eve—Very sick.

3rd: Company came in from picket. Some firing on the lines. One of our men was shot in the foot. The Captain gave me a blowing because I did not go on picket. I told him I would resign.

4th: Sick. In quarters all day. Eve—In tent. I do not feel well and kind of mad.

5th: Very sick in tent. The doctor came to see me.

6th: Uneasy night. The Regt. was out at three in the morning on scout. The company was out scouting all day but not a Rebel could they find. The boys are very mad about it.

7th: Sick all day. The doctor gave me some pills.

8th: Sunday. Very sick. Very pleasant outdoors. It is hard for me to stay inside.

9th: Another pleasant day. Regt. is at skirmish drill and sham fighting. Such a roaring of guns I cannot rest.

10th: Doctor came down and he was mad because I would not come to him at surgery call. I told him I would when possible.

11th: Boys all gone on picket. Long roll beat twice through the day. I was ready to turn out for a fight. I feel some better.

12th: Boys came home all sound except one who got the measles.

13th: I tattooed some on the cook's arm. A fine day. All quiet.

14th: Boys fixed up the street. I wrote a letter home. Eve—We caught a man dressed in woman's clothes.

15th: Sunday. I wrote a letter to Ralph Hoyt. Read all the news. Eve—I received a letter from home.

16th: Heavy cannonading off south all day. Our company on scout.

17th: The Mayor of Buffalo was here and some members of Congress. Our Regt. did some big shooting.

18th: Haines came in as a tent mate. We had a dispute on the weight of water and milk.

19th: I pass the day reading and *thinking about going to the Rocky Mountains as soon as I am discharged.*

20th: The long roll beat at twelve and all were marched to

Dranesville. We crossed the lines five miles, using our Regiment as support while General McCall had a sharp fight. 60 killed on the Rebel side, 12 on our side.

21st: McCall went out again this morning with his division for a fight, but all is quiet.

22nd: I was on scout and got cut off between the lines. I was spying on an officer riding a white horse in the lower end of a clearing and was detected by the enemy. They were not long waking me to the fact but I made my escape in a shower of rifle balls with only a scratch and my cap shot from my head.

23rd: We have been losing a man about every night on the advance picket, a very dangerous post. I am ordered to investigate. A moonlight night. I take one man with me and camp on a little knoll behind a fence.

24th: At 3 in the morning we heard a noise in the edge of the woods. It sounded like a hog. I whispered to my partner, "Be ready to shoot when I say the word." I saw something move and I told him, "Aim low and fire." Bang! went our guns. The hog grunting stopped and the groaning began and quite a commotion in the brush. We think there will be no more trouble on this post.

25th: Christmas. A number of the Erie boys were over to see me. I treated them on oysters. Eve—Great fireworks in Co. B. The brass band played splendidly. A good deal of fun.

26th: A good deal of talk about electing a Lieut. and getting up a band.

27th: Quiet. Dull.

28th: The horns came for the band. I talk strongly of joining them. I think it would be better for me.

29th: Sunday. More talk about going into the band. In fact I go join it. Dutch Charley is instructor and Drum Major. As I have been acting as bugler for skirmish drill Charley discovered I could play a cornet and was bent on getting me detailed. He did unbeknownst to my Capt., and I just packed and moved to band headquarters. My Capt. got mad and sent a guard of soldiers to fetch me, but I told the boys I could not come and to tell the

Capt. I said so. And up to the Colonel he went raving about how I had disobeyed orders. The old Colonel told him quietly that I was all right and had been put on detached duty for this work. The Captain's feathers dropped and he had no more to say.

30th: In the band room. We practiced all day. All did well for the first time. It made my lips somewhat sore. Eve—Some talk about advancing and one thing or another.

31st: A good deal of firing going on. The 21st Band came at 12 o'clock and gave us a serenade and they got tight and got to fighting amongst themselves. A great time.

January 1st, 1862: Up to the band tent practicing. Not a word said about last night.

2nd: Up to the band tent. Capt. said I should return to the company. I told him I was in the Band.

3rd: Up to the band tent. All did well. Our bass drum came. Our Capt. is rather mad at me.

4th: I feel very sick and took six pills. It snows. Eve—To band tent practicing. I feel weak..

5th: Sunday. Up to band tent. We learned Old Hundred.

6th: We went to work and built a shanty to practice and sleep in.

7th: Worked on the shanty. Rather cold. Some talk about payday.

8th: We got paid. I got $34.

9th: Up to band quarters. Very muddy. Half the Regt. is drunk. Great time.

10th: At band room all day practicing. Some talk about advancing.

11th: I was taken sick with cholera and had to send for the doctor on the double quick. Two hours I lay in agony. The doctor gave me chloroform.

12th: Sunday. I was taken again and laid ten hours in great pain. I took two large doses of salts and one of castor oil. It relieved me at eight at night and I went to sleep.

13th: At 4 A.M. my physic relieved me and I feel better but am very weak. The doctor says my liver is infected.

14th: Very weak. It hurts me to walk. I cannot set up.

15th: I am about the same. The doctor ordered three quinine pills a day.

16th: About the same. The band is improving fast. It makes me feel bad that I am not able to practice with them. The quarter-master was in to hear them play.

17th: I can sit up but only for a little while at a time. Oh, I feel bad.

18th: It rained all day. All mud in our tent. It is enough to make a well man sick. There is no place like home. I think of home.

19th: Sunday. Very muddy. I went down to our Company and got a piece of liver for dinner. I feel better.

20th: I feel a great deal better. The 87th came over. Oh so muddy—they are all covered. All tight too. We took one into our quarters. He is sick and cold and wet.

21st: I went down and saw Sammie. Played bluff a little while. Eve—Down to Sammie's house in the woods and lost $15. We had a good deal of fun.

22nd: I took first alto to play. It is not so hard for me. I am very weak.

23rd: I feel very sleepy. I mean to sleep all day except for practice. Eve—To bed early.

24th: It snows and rains. Very muddy. I feel very well. I am resigned to the ranks.

25th: Very cold. We went out in the field and practiced. Eve—Practicing.

26th: Sunday. Ground is frozen hard. We played on parade.

27th: We practiced on parade ground. I bought a revolver and traded it for a watch.

28th: Practiced as usual. Eve—Down to the house and played cards. A good deal of fun.

29th: I came into camp just at morning. Very sleepy. Practiced as usual.

30th: Down to Sammie's house. Some officers and guards came and arrested the whole of us. They did not get me. A Lieut.

came in with the lantern leaving a guard at the door. I took in the situation at a glance and dropped the visor of my cap and pulled up my coat collar so I would not be recognized. The boys were all flustered and rose from the table leaving quite a pile of money so I just scraped it up and put it in my pocket and followed the officer to the door. As he turned to make a search upstairs I dropped a gold piece and exclaimed, "I have lost a twenty! Whoever finds it can have it." The officer stooped with his lantern and the guard neglected his duty to help look for it. I accepted their offer and jumped out the door. They jumped after me and hollered "Halt!" and fired a close shot but I was already making time down the hill through the small pines. Then came a volley with no results except to make me go faster. I took through the timber crossing our inside picket line and back to quarters. My band mates greeted me with "For God's sake, Joe, where have you been? The Rebs must have been after you hot this time." I should say so—for I was mud from head to foot and my clothes were half gone and in rags but I said, "Boys, mum is the word," and cleaned up and went to bed.

31st: Not a peep about last night. The officers do not know who escaped.

[Snow and rain continued into February, the fifth month of McClellan's preparations. Hoyt spent his time "practicing, playing bluff, and writing letters home." On February 7, the regiment received new rifles. On the thirteenth came news of the success of Burnside's expedition: "Captured 3000 and killed 1000 in Tennessee." The band played.]

February 20th: Great things stirring. The 77th New York Volunteers joined our division on the 15th. The 33rd New York, Colonel Taylor; 43rd New York, Colonel Vinton; 49th Pennsylvania, Colonel Irwin; 6th Maine, Colonel Knowles, and the 5th Wisconsin, Colonel Cobb, now compose the third brigade, all under the command of General Hancock. Our second brigade is composed entirely of Vermont troops, including the 2nd, 3rd, 4th, 5th and 6th Vermont Regiments, and nobly do they sustain the reputation of the Green Mountain Boys.

[On February 26, there was "some talk of advancing.... Looks like a more active life for me now." Hoyt went back to his company "for I can see the band business has about had its day. Even my Capt. is glad to see me on duty once more." On March 5, "we got orders to march."]

March 6th: Routed out at one A.M. with 24 hour rations. At daybreak we were in Dranesville. At eight o'clock we were at Vienna in sight of the Rebels. We skirmished all day and came back with one prisoner.

7th: Very sore and lame. We had to go on Brigade drill. Oh such swearing I never heard.

8th: Practiced on the bugle. We played for guard mounting. Co. G and Co. B are elected as skirmishers. Eve—One of God's nights—so pleasant.

9th: Weaver and I went down in the woods and practiced the bugle. I told the boys we would move in the morning. They laughed at me. Eve—Another splendid night.

10th: We were routed out at one o'clock. Great hustling around camp. We arrived in Vienna at 10 o'clock. *The whole Army of the Potomac is on the move.* We drove the Rebels before us. Eve—In Fairfax. The Rebels all run for their lives.

11th: A hard night. So very cold. We remained all day expecting to meet the enemy. Our cavalry went into Bull Run, but the Rebels have all retreated and blown up Manassas Junction and burned Centreville. I went on scout and brought in one prisoner and made him double quick into camp carrying his flag. Such cheering I never heard.

12th: We understand McClellan is going to examine Bull Run today. Brigade out drilling. McClellan is expected to review us.

13th: In the afternoon we are reviewed by McClellan. Great cheering. He makes good promises.

14th: In camp at Flint Hill. We are getting ready for a long march. We think we are going down the coast.

CHAPTER V

From Flint Hill to the Chickahominy— The Peninsular Campaign of 1862

[The early Union disasters so sobered the people and the press that General McClellan had been given a free hand almost to the point of military dictatorship. As the year drew to a close, however, with the army swollen to 189,000, the roads in fine condition, and the troops eager to move forward, the people again demanded action. Still nothing happened. The large force on the Potomac lay idle, the expenses mounted, and foreign governments grew more and more threatening. Chafing at the intolerable situation, Congress began an inquiry into the conduct of the war, and a council was called by the President at the White House. It was decided that a successful attack could be made, that the army could descend the Potomac to Chesapeake Bay, enter the Rappahannock, land at Urbana on the western bank, push across the country to West Point, at the head of York River, and threaten Richmond from that direction before General Johnston and his Confederate forces could reach them, at the same time keeping sufficient troops intact to render a counterattack on Washington impossible. Weeks passed with still no action from McClellan. Losing his patience, President Lincoln issued War Order No. 1, dated January 27, 1862, setting February 22 as the day for a general movement by land and sea. The delay continued; there was more consultation and a second council of war, in which it

49

was finally agreed to accept McClellan's plan to attack by way of the lower Chesapeake and up the peninsula. On March 8, the President issued a new war order naming March 18 as the day for opening the campaign. Immediately—for reasons unknown— McClellan had ordered his troops to occupy Manassas and Centreville. It was then learned that the grim row of 100-pound Parrott guns that had defied the Union army all winter were a sham—no more than huge logs with round black spots painted on the ends to represent muzzles. It was more humiliating to the North than the defeat at Bull Run, and added to the disenchantment with McClellan. On March 11, the President relieved him as General-in-Chief of the armies, placed him in charge of the Richmond campaign, and shifted General Halleck in the West to department command. There is no doubt that the Confederates learned of the Union plans as fast as they were made, for within twenty-four hours after abandoning Manassas and Centreville, Johnston's army pushed toward Richmond, taking up a strong position on the south bank of the Rappahannock. This had necessitated a change of base. Fortress Monroe had been decided upon, instead of Urbana. The objective was the same—the Confederate capital.]

March 15th: Up early and off for Alexandria—20 miles. Rain all day. Saw some secessionist prisoners as we passed through Fairfax. Eve—Encamped about 3 miles from Alexandria. Very tired and wet.

16th: Sunday. Feel rather stiff from standing in water all night. The rain came down in chunks. We had to stand up to keep from being drowned. Kept a good fire all day and dried ourselves. All very anxious to move.

17th: Hurt in the woods but feel all right. A nice day. Went up the hill and had a far view of Alexandria.

18th: All very anxious to leave. Regt. had drill in the afternoon. Cooks have drawn five days' rations and I think we will go soon.

19th: Very rainy and wet. We have to move our tents up into the field. We are all mad about it.

Buckskin Joe

20th: Benchly and I went down to Alexandria on an old pass. I found out where Dutch Charley could get our instruments fixed. Had a good deal of fun. Very rainy.

21st: Some talk about moving. Very muddy.

22nd: Charley took our instruments to Alexandria to get them fixed. Weaver and I took a walk in the woods. We shot at a mark. Very muddy.

23rd: Sunday. Three cheers. We got marching orders. We struck tents and off we go to Alexandria. Here we took the steamboats for Fortress Monroe. Eve—We anchored at Mt. Vernon and all went to bed on deck. Very chilly. Very pleasant scenery down the river.

24th: Off early. We amuse ourselves looking at strange objects as we cross Chesapeake Bay. Eve—We laid at the docks of Fortress Monroe all night, but glad to have got to our journey's end.

25th: Up early and left the boats. We marched to Hampton and up Hampton Roads four miles and encamped. We can see the Rebels on the other side of the James River.

26th: In camp here all day. A splendid place. A great many rumors around camp. We are ready for a fight.

27th: We were routed out for a skirmish. We drove the Rebels before us to Little Bethel and they burned it. Eve—We planted our batteries and camped on the site of Little Bethel. We killed some cattle to eat.

28th: Up early. All quiet. A good many skins and critter heads hanging on the trees. We went back to Newport News for provisions and encamped here for the night once more.

29th: I went down to Newport News and saw where the *Cumberland* and the *Congress* were sunk by the *Merrimac,* and the little *Monitor* that whipped the *Merrimac* and also Colonel Snow's headquarters that was shot to pieces in this fight. I can see the Rebel flag on the other side.

30th: Sunday. Very rainy and muddy. The general moved our camp up onto the beach. A nice place. I received a letter from home notifying me that Aaron Whittier is in the 3rd Vermont. I am surprised. I will go see him tomorrow.

31st: I went down and found Whittier. We were very pleased to see each other. We were taking a walk along the river bank and saw a Rebel gunboat slipping down the other side. About 1000 of our boys were in swimming. It threw three shells at us and one solid shot and did no damage but the boys sure came out of that water naked, grabbing their clothes and running for camp. Down the beach came our flying artillery and swung into line returning the fire and the gunboat retreated. Whittier and I hid behind some apple trees. The fight didn't last long. It was short and sweet—like a roasted maggot.

April 1st: Our brigade went out on scout. We found Rebels this side of Little Bethel but we shelled them out and took one woman spy. We got back and our Col. was taken sick on the way.

2nd: All day some firing at our troops as they came into Fortress Monroe but no damage done.

3rd: Brook's Brigade moved up into line with us. Orders were read on dress parade for a march. Great cheering. All feel well.

4th: We advanced at eight and drove the Rebels before us from Young's Mills and burned up their winter quarters. Eve— Encamped here.

5th: Up early and drove the enemy to the mouth of York River. Here they are very strongly fortified. Hard fighting all day. The 49th lost one killed and one wounded. Eve—On our arms all night.

6th: Up early and at it again. They tried to shell us out but could not. Great excitement. The ball and shell whistle like hail. We lost a good many wounded and killed—first a poor fellow from the 7th Maine, his heart and lung torn out by a shell. I was standing ten feet away, and his lungs and flesh nearly knocked me down and I was blinded by blood. I saw General McClellan dismount here and sight his cannon and cut the Rebel flag down in their fort twice out of three shots. He laughed and said, "Boys, that is the way to do it!" then mounted and rode off.

7th: The firing is steady on both sides. Showers of grape

and canister fall in our camp. They become so familiar that only the fiercest volleys alarm us.

8th: We worked all night throwing up breastworks in a shower of bullets. They would come in volleys and at the flash of Rebel guns we would drop to the ground allowing the shots to pass. Then we were up and at it again. We had the breastwork completed by morning and a rifle pit all the way across the field right under their noses. Berdan's sharpshooters occupy the rifle pit with Motts and Ayers battery on the right. The Rebel pit is directly across from us on the opposite side of a small stream [Warwick River] and directly under the fort occupied by the Mississippi sharpshooters. Each side have sandbags protecting their heads and shoot at anything and everything in sight.

9th: A stray rifleman started picking off our men. I was not long locating him in a hollow tree off to the right. He had cut a hole in the trunk to fire through and, being inside, no doubt considered himself safe. I sent word to the battery to turn on the tree. The first shot ran him out and he was riddled by bullets.

10th: I was with the Major of the 33rd inspecting the breastworks and looking through his field glasses at a porthole in the Rebel fort. I saw a flash and moved just in time for the ball to pass under my arm cutting the threads of my coat. "That's what I call dodging a bullet," the Major said. "That is what I call a damned close call," said I. As the old lady remarked when the wheel barrow ran over her nose, it was sharp work for the eyes.

11th: I was on picket and stuck my head and shoulders a little too far from behind a tree in the moonlight when quick as a flash a rifle fired from behind a log. I disappeared just as quickly and the Johnny obviously believed he had killed another Yank and was correspondingly happy and proud. It was his chagrin a few minutes later to hear: "I say, Reb, have you got any tobacco to trade for coffee?" After a while he answered: "I have 'baccy and if you have coffee we can make a dicker," and with these words he showed himself just enough that I got a shot that cut a hole in his hat and shaved off a lock of his hair. He dropped back behind his log and we argued the case. Finally I went off and got the coffee and the Johnny got the tobacco, and after tying our handkerchiefs to our ramrods we met each other. He introduced himself as William Palmer, known in his native Texas as "Butcher-knife Bill," and I told him I was Ed Hoyt, late of New York, better known as Buckskin Joe.

12th: The Rebel attacks come more often. The rumor is that old Jeff Davis has told us to get out of this place or he will help us out. We defy him to undertake it. Bullets whiz through the camp and our tents all the time. One of our boys was eating when a bullet hit his plate. Such threats and oaths I never heard and I left him scraping up his beans, dirt and all.

13th: The 20th New York joined us. They have never smelled powder and were ordered to learn the skirmish drill. The Colonel, a German, commenced as follows: " 'Tention, battalion. Now, boys, ve must do mit dey call de skermish. I don't know him mach but dey scatter awa'—six mid a bunch all along de line little ways apart. 'Tention, battalion, prepare to scatter. Scatter!" And they ran and gathered into groups in a long line. "Dot must be well don, I tinks, boys, so we quit for further orders. Break ranks, march."

14th: The 20th were detailed to go on picket and relieve us. Now here goes for a good night's sleep—a treat for all. But the Johnnys were not long discovering the change and made a charge in the night, and the 20th broke and ran like a stampede. The long roll brought us out of dreamland and into line half asleep. The musketry became fierce and our bullets were soon singing that old familiar tune. The 20th redeemed themselves. They came back in a quick advance and we charged with a yell and a volley and the Rebels went back in a hurry, leaving us at the old stand.

15th: The flag of truce was raised to give both sides a chance to bury the dead. While the flag was up the Rebels and our boys filled the trees trying to get a look at each other—a little too far apart to spit tobacco juice and not daring to shoot. When the flag was lowered those men sure dropped out of those trees.

16th: We were ordered to make an assault. Something happened that I cannot account for unless it was bad whiskey.

Two companies of the 3rd Vermont were ordered forward. Down the hill they came, rushed into the water and made for the rifle pits. They gained the first line of works then the second. A ditch to their left was filled with Rebels. They poured a volley into them and the Rebels fled. Actually the fort was in their possession but when they looked for support no order came. The Rebels cut the dam loose above and the poor boys were forced to retreat through the raging water in a constant shower of bullets. My friend Whittier was in the fracas and I counted 21 bullet holes in his overcoat rolled on his knapsack. He never got a scratch but his company was nearly cut to pieces.

17th: Worked hard building new breastworks. Heavy firing all night. The Rebels tried to cross the creek. The guns roar and the shells and balls whistle.

18th: We moved our camp close to the fort—a devil of a time.

19th: Sharp firing on picket lines all day. Eve—Out all night on reserve. Oh how the balls whistle around us. We give them fits.

20th: We moved down to support our batteries in the breastworks. Very rainy and wet all day. Eve—Firing on the lines.

21st: Behind our breastworks viewing the Rebel fort. A flag of truce is raised at 8 P.M. We see plenty of Rebels working on their fort while the flag is up. We are very mad about it. At 3 A.M. the flag came down and firing commenced.

22nd: Behind our breastworks. The Rebels are still working and skulking. I saw their sharpshooters come into the rifle pits. They shot so close we had to leave the field. They shot three times at me. They tried to drive our pickets in. The 7th Maine had quite a fight, took one prisoner.

23rd: We worked all night cutting out the timber for our big guns. Our sharpshooters are busy all day shooting the Rebels and occasionally have a shell thrown at them. Eve—I can hear the Rebel band playing. We are all very anxious to have a showdown. Victory or death our motto.

24th: Very heavy cannonading. I caught a spy but the General let him go. 7th Maine drove the Rebel pickets in. I went into our breastworks with our sharpshooters. Had fun all day dodging balls.

25th: Heavy cannonading. One of our sergeants got shot. I hear that the Col. and Major of the 93rd Regt. have deserted. Eve—Heavy firing toward Yorktown.

26th: Rainy. Heavy firing toward Yorktown. Professor Gow is here with his balloon. We are all very uneasy. We want to advance. We expect a hard fight.

27th: Sunday. Heavy firing on the lines. Eve—We got our pay and all feel better.

28th: I went around and squared with the Regt. I have $46. I sent $40 home. Brigade had quite a fight. Over 200 Rebels killed.

29th: Down to our breastworks. They are fixing to plant more big guns.

30th: Heavy firing all night. News is that old Beauregard has surrendered at Corinth.

May 1st: Up early and had some pudding for breakfast. I feel rather cross. Pony Freeman was buried. Report is that 500 Rebels gave themselves up last evening. Eve—It lightens off in the west. All quiet on the lines.

2nd: Ambulance Corps helped the doctor fix up around the hospital. I received a letter from home. I wrote a letter to Warren. Two mortars were taken into the field.

3rd: We planted our mortars and are ready for execution. Heavy cannonading toward Yorktown. A hot day. Our Adjutant is very sick. Heavy cannonading off to our right.

4th: Sunday. Three cheers. The Rebels have evacuated. We drew in our pickets and packed up and away we go after them. Oh, such strong fortifications I never seen. They had a good many torpedoes planted for us but they did not amount to much. We dug them up. We drove the Rebels before us all day. Eve— Encamped three miles from Williamsburg in a big wheat field. Very rainy and cold all night. We learned that the Rebels are going to make a stand.

5th: The battle was commenced early in the morning by our cavalry in the woods. We had hard fighting all day. Our division took three forts. McClellan came and we all had to double quick onto the battlefield. Oh, such a sight. We took a hundred and fifty prisoners. The Rebels have evacuated and retreated with our troops after them. We had to lag back to take care of the dead and wounded. We camped by the fort and it rained all night.

6th: Up at daybreak, cold, wet and hungry, for our supply trains are stuck in the mud far behind us. I took a couple of haversacks and went onto the battlefield and robbed the dead Johnnys of their hard biscuit then went back to the woods and woke my mess mates for breakfast. They soon discovered what I had done but we were hungry enough to eat a dog raw.

7th: Worked all day lugging the wounded off the field and burying the dead.

8th: We dug long trenches and piled them in—but a good many were burned in the swamps.

9th: Our supply trains caught up and we moved on through Williamsburg. I shall never forget the comments from the women in the town as we passed. "Oh," they said, "you will soon be going back faster than you are going up."

10th: Up and off for Richmond. Very warm. We took our time. At two we were in Barhamsville. Our troops at the head had a brush at West Point. Eve—We stopped two miles from West Point. We hear heavy cannonading on the river.

11th: Sunday. Up and on we go for our Regt. We cut across country and found our Regt. encamped six miles above West Point. We had a great time buying hoecakes from niggers and paying them in Confederate script. Eve—In camp with my Regt. just above the Point.

12th: In camp all day. I feel hard up. We went out and practiced a little. We played for parade. I wrote a letter home.

13th: All up and off for Richmond again. We went to Cumberland Landing and encamped. A great many troops here. All quiet on the lines. I went swimming in the river.

14th: Up and off. We went four miles to Whitehouse Landing and encamped on the Pamunkey River, 20 miles from Richmond. I went down and saw where the Rebels burned the railroad bridge.

15th: Rainy day. Benchly and I went down to the dock and caught enough fish for a meal. A good many gunboats here at the Landing. We expect a fight soon.

16th: In camp all day. Rainy. I do not feel well. My liver and kidneys trouble me. No appetite. My back is very bad. But I will not complain—we are McClellan's reserve.

17th: We had marching orders and packed up and marched out, but the order was countermanded and we went back into camp. I feel very bad.

18th: Sunday. I am very weak and sick. Our band broke up. I was detailed to play a fife in the drum corps. I think of home.

19th: Marching orders—up early and off for Richmond. We went eight miles and encamped on the main road. It is hard for me to march. I am weak and sick.

20th: Up at two and off again. I went to the doctor and he gave me some quinine. I feel very bad. On the main road.

21st: Up and off. Encamped at Coal Harbor and our balloon went up. I feel very sick.

22nd: Very sick. I went to see the doctor. He told me to take quinine three times a day. I gave a dollar for the use of a dollar till payday.

23rd: Heavy cannonading on our right. We had orders to march but I was so sick I could not go. The balloon went up a number of times. Our troops drove their pickets in. Eve—They are in the swamps.

24th: I went up to see the doctor. It begins to rain. Our Brigade had a skirmish. Oh, I feel very anxious to be able to go with them.

25th: Sunday. Our Regt. is within five miles of Richmond. Our Brigade drove them out of Mechanicsville. Had quite a little fight. Wheeler's battery and the 77th New York did some good work here. Surprised them early in the morning and so suddenly they left a stand of firearms back of a large brick house. A young lady music teacher was inside playing a piano. A solid shot passed through the wall and went through her piano endways.

26th: We drove the Rebels across the Chickahominy yesterday. I went back to the Regt. but I feel very unwell. At Mechanicsville.

27th: We went back two miles and encamped in a field. I bought some meal and tried to cook something I could eat.

28th: McClellan gave us orders to make ready for a hard fight for we are going into Richmond in a few days. Every man is to have 20 rounds in his pockets and 40 in his cartridge box. I am very sick.

29th: I feel a little better. I hope and pray that nature will cure me for it is all I trust in. I will die before I will go to our doctor again. How I would like to shoot him.

30th: The Rebels are coming in every day and giving themselves up—almost starved. I feel a little stronger. I try to be well but cannot. I cannot sleep at night. I am in such pain.

31st: I begin to get discouraged. I am weaker. I want to see our Brigade surgeon. Lamb and the Lieut. came up to see me. I think I will not live long. Hard fighting on our left all day.

June 1st: I am weaker than ever. I saw Lamb and our Capt. Our Capt. got the doctor.

2nd: I am just alive, and that is all. Oh, how I want to get well. I got a letter from home. I am sorry to hear of my grandfather's death. Oh, if I could only be home now. God help me.

3rd: It has been rain, thunder, and lightning the last four days and nights. I feel better by spells but awful sick.

4th: The doctor came to see me. I am so weak I can hardly stand. Oh, such a beastly doctor.

5th: The Regt. advanced across the Chickahominy. I crawled on my hands and knees to go but could not. The stream is all out of its banks, and our army seems on the point of annihilation from disease and chronic diarrhea. More of our men are disabled here by sickness than by the enemy. My Lieut. picked me up out of the swamps and hired a team and sent me to the hospital to die. Hank Weaver came and took care of me. I think I have typhoid fever.

6th: Weaver is doing all he can for me. The doctor came to see us and took our names.

7th: I am no better. Oh, home, my home! If I could only get home. I cannot live long.

8th: Sunday. I thought it would be best for me to leave this tent to break the fever. Hank put up a tent out of some boards and I got under them. I have the typhoid sure.

9th: I am in awful pain. I am wholly dependent on Hank.

10th: I cannot live long. I would apply for my discharge if I thought it would do any good.

11th: My Capt. came with my descriptive list. I am bound to keep my courage.

12th: I had two ulcerated sores gather in my head and break.

13th: My head feels a great deal better but my eyes and back are very weak. I have taken three different kinds of pills to break my fever, which is all that will save me.

14th: Nothing I eat agrees with me. My bowels are very bad.

15th: Sunday. I have to go as usual. Hank went off after some vegetables.   Rained hard.

16th: Good deal of pain in my bowels. I am afraid of rheumatism.

17th: About the same. A good deal of pain in my hips and back.

18th: I think I am some better. The doctor thinks I must go north or I will die.

19th: We were all examined and a good many sent north. My name was taken to go. I expect to go tomorrow.

20th: Hank looks after me. I would die if it wasn't for Hank.

21st: The Rebels fired into two of our hospitals and drove the sick into the woods. An awful thing. 300 sick go to Whitehouse Landing. I do not go yet.

22nd: Sunday. I start for Whitehouse Landing in ambulance. We arrived at midnight. Oh, such a time at the station. I was in the car when the engine ran into it and was thrown 20 feet down an embankment in the dark. The supplies destroyed are beyond my calculation. I crawled into the car while they were getting the engine back on the track.

23rd: We arrived at the landing at 2 A.M. and took the boat for New York. Eve—We arrived at Fortress Monroe and anchored and stayed all night.

24th: We cannot start until 10 the sea is so rough. A good many of the boys are very sick—sea sick. My bowels pain me very much. Eve—I run all night, I cannot sleep. I no longer care what becomes of the army or myself.

CHAPTER VI

Out of the Hospital and Back to My Regiment—From the Battlefield to Portsmouth Grove, Rhode Island—An Attempt on My Life by an Army Doctor and My Escape to Canada '

[The last six months of Mr. Hoyt's diary is largely devoted to his experience in government hospitals and is often repetitious. He best describes the events of his period in his biography]:

I arrived in New York City on June 25 and was taken to the New York barracks with the 300 sick. Here they washed us, gave us clean clothes, and got rid of our graybacks. Then we were separated. Most of the boys went to the government hospital for treatment, furlough, and discharge. I was taken with the more dangerous cases to the city hospital. The head physician examined me and said I had inflamation of the bowels. He was doubtful of my recovery.

I took the medicine he gave me, gargled regularly with stuff that turned my mouth and tongue black, kept a flaxseed poultice on my bowels to relieve the soreness, and ate nothing but mush and milk for days. I really had a siege of it. It was mid-July before I was able to stand or walk straight or sit at the table for my meals.

When I was able to be up and around, I was never so lonesome in my life. I wrote letters home and to my friends in the regiment, and received some. I passed the rest of the time walking the floor, looking through the iron gates and reading the news of the war. I tried to get a furlough and was turned down because the doctor said I was in no condition to travel.

On July 21, all of us were moved upstairs to a new ward to make room for a great number of sick and wounded who arrived next day. It was more pleasant here, but I was still cooped up in that devilish hospital.

On the 25th, three of us went to No. 6 State Street to get our pay. Afterwards we were allowed the run of the yard, and I bought some good brandy over the fence. That evening I was taken with terrible cramps in the stomach. The doctor came and put me to bed. I had to take castor oil and twenty drops of laudanum for my bowels. He drew a blister over my liver to relieve my distress. A mustard seed poultice was applied. On the 30th, he ordered a strengthening plaster on my back, and I felt better. Finally I was allowed down in the yard again. I thought about jumping the fence and going into the city. I was at a standstill. I did not know what to do nor what course to take.

On August 4, I read the news that they were going to draft men for federal service. [General Lee now commanded the Confederate army. General McClellan's forces had been halted before Richmond and driven back to Harrison's Bar with a loss of thousands taken prisoner, killed, or wounded. The Army of the Potomac had been split in two, with the entire force of the enemy between them. To unite by land was a physical impossibility. General Halleck had ordered the army withdrawn from the peninsula and transported by water to a new base on the Rappahannock at Fredericksburg, thus bringing it within sixty miles of Richmond and securing the reinforcement of 40,000 to 50,000 fresh and disciplined troops. McClellan objected and had been relieved of his command. The separate forces of McDowell, Fremont, and Banks were now consolidated into one organization, called the Army of Virginia, under General John Pope, Halleck's most efficient subordinate from the West. Long before this, however, it had become apparent in Washington that the Union armies must be largely increased. The conscription act of the Confederacy had filled its ranks with fresh troops. Prompt action was needed, and on August 4, President Lincoln issued a call for a second army of 300,000 three-year men.] I told the doctor that if they needed men that bad he had better send me back to my regiment. He told me I had better take a discharge. I told him I did not want it, but that I would take a furlough. He said, "All furloughs have been cancelled." I made up my mind then that I was going to get back into the fight.

On the 22nd, General Corcoran arrived in New York City, and I got a pass to go down to see him. I never seen such a crowd on Broadway. I ran into some of the boys I knew from the 77th; we raised the devil all day and wound up at Fort Hamilton in the night all tuckered out. They had joined a squad detailed for the front, and I decided to go with them. Some hospital guards came looking for me, but I got away on the boat the next morning, went to Long Island, and boarded the train for Washington.

We arrived in Washington at 8 o'clock and scattered, each man for himself. I went to Alexandria, where I ran into one of my old officers just as he was starting for the front, and went with him. At Fredericksburg, on August 31, I discovered my doctor knew more than I did. I was picked up on the battlefield, nearly dead from exhaustion, and taken back to Alexandria with the wounded. This time I was shipped to the government hospital at Portsmouth Grove, Rhode Island.

I could tell of a hundred things that happened here, but they would not look well in history. I will say this—the sick and wounded were treated like dogs by one of the most beastly army doctors I ever encountered. I saw him experiment on one soldier with a crooked back who was under the influence of chloroform; he tried to straighten his back by standing and jumping on him. He took another soldier's shirt away from him because he had two. I saw men forced to clean out privies, chop wood, and work on the road to the burying ground when they were not able. On November 27, we were all set to have a turkey dinner—the first decent meal we had eaten in months—but our devilish doctor took the turkey away from us. The boys rioted in the mess hall, and they had to call out all the guards to stop us. Many landed in the guardhouse. Others were put on work details in the cold and snow. At least one attempt was made to kill this doctor. I think I would have shot him myself if I had been given the opportunity.

I tried to get a furlough, twice I applied for a discharge, but that is all the good it did. The doctor found out that I had not been paid in five months, and just before payday, he detailed me to go aboard an old ship bound for God knows where. He refused to give me my descriptive list, and I concluded that he intended to draw my money for himself and dispose of me. I talked it over with some of the boys, and they advised me to run away if I wanted to save my life.

On December 1, I packed my things. The boat was due at 3 P.M. At noon I left the barracks in the rain, getting through the guard with an old pass. I did not go to the docks. As soon as I reached the railroad, I lit out down the tracks, and ran two miles before I stopped to rest. Then I headed north for Tiverton, reaching some old fishing shanties that night.

I now needed someone I could trust to help me make my escape. I selected a fisherman's wife. I told her my story, and she agreed not to betray me. She gave me a room upstairs, and I stayed there all night. The next morning she brought me a fisherman's suit, but just as I was in the process of getting rid of my uniform, the patrols came to the lower part of the house inquiring about me. I opened a door leading out from above and jumped. I made it to the hogpen and hid in the hog shed. They searched the house and went on.

It was dark before I came back and changed clothes. When I was ready to leave, the good lady gave me a bottle of whiskey and a kiss, wished me Godspeed, and I struck for Fall River with the intention of crossing in a boat. The boats were locked, so I struck for the bridge and discovered a lookout in the moonlight. He was standing on the bridge, reading a newspaper. I accepted his offer and worked my way into the shadows, moving quietly through the water, directly beneath him, and reached the other side safely. With the coast clear ahead, I made it to Fall River City.

I did not know the country and had only two dollars in my pocket. I passed through the city to the first station on the railroad

[Bowenville], entered an old barn, and slept in a horse stall the rest of the night. At daylight I walked down to the station, where I took the first look at myself in my new costume. Well, I was a holy fright. As soon as the train came, I boarded it and went into the second-class car, and mingled with a gang of Irish workmen. After paying my fare to Boston, I had seventy-five cents.

I arrived in Boston at 10 A.M. and waited at the depot until evening with nothing to eat. My seventy-five cents took me to Manchester. I tried to continue, and they put me off the train, so I took the road to Lowell on foot. That night I stopped with a farmer and sold him my watch for $5. The next morning I boarded the stage to Lowell. I had $2 left. My feet were sore and in blisters and I had to have shoes. I bought a pair for a dollar and used the balance for a ticket to North Enfield, New Hampshire, arriving late at night.

I spotted an old hotel on a hill. It was dark and quiet, but I went to the place and knocked. I saw a lady coming with a lamp, through the window, and when she opened the door, I told her I was cold and hungry, that by hard luck I had lost my money and needed a place to sleep.

"That is all right," she said. "Come right in, and I will fix you something to eat." So I made myself at home. "Where are you from?" she asked.

"Madam," said I, "I am from the Army of the Potomac."

"Why," said she, "my husband is a Captain in that Army. Have you been discharged?"

"No, madam, I was with a sutler outfit. They were all captured but me, and I am trying to get home to Vermont," I lied.

"Oh," she said, "you can stay here as long as you want and work for me."

I accepted her hospitality for the night. I bathed my sore feet with a little whiskey and landed in the center of a feather bed, thinking what a glorious sleep I would have. But I had nothing but aches and pains, roll and tumble, and finally was forced to get up, take a quilt, and roll up on the floor. To show what habit will do, I was at once in dreamland.

The next morning I thanked her and started north in a snow storm—I knew better than to hang around town long, and an old Canadian friend of mine, Thomas Watt, lived near North Enfield. A few miles out, I came upon a little house and a man chopping wood in the snow. As I approached him, he dropped his ax, and exclaimed: "In the name of God, Joe, where did you come from? I thought you were in the Army."

"I was, Tom, but I lack right smart of it now. I am on a strike for higher wages and better grub and treatment."

"Well, come in," he said, "and where did you get them duds?"

I told him a sweet lady had given them to me. "They don't fit so well, but they are more profitable just now." Then I explained what it was all about, and we held a council of war, for I expected they would be after me. There was a big reward for deserters. He took me to Lebanon as his hired man from Canada and bought me a new suit of clothes, a shave, and a haircut. I was so disfigured now that I had to ask myself who I was when I looked in a glass.

A few days later, Tom reported they were after me, that a detective had traced me to the hotel in North Enfield, and I would have to make for Canada. On December 22, I bid him good-bye. With his old fiddle under my arm and a pistol in my belt, I went to a little station called Carson and boarded the train for Barton Landing, Vermont. As I passed through North Enfield, I noticed a man get on the train who eyed me constantly, but I put on a bold front.

I arrived at Barton Landing safe and sound, and from there caught the stage thirty miles to Derby Line where it crossed the river onto the Stanstead Plains in the Province of Quebec. Two ladies and the man got into the Concord coach with me. The ladies were bound for Canada. The man made no comment about his destination.

It was a tedious ride, very bad wheeling, for the roads were icy, but we stood it nicely, reaching the line about dark. We got off the stage and waited in the hotel for our baggage to be searched before crossing. I got out my fiddle, cocked my feet on the stove, and otherwise made myself so familiar that the gentleman making the inspection said nothing to me. But I kept one hand near my gun and my eye on every move of my strange passenger-companion, for there was only the river between me and safety.

When the word came, "All aboard," I leisurely left the hotel and entered the stage on the side opposite the stranger. It was only a short distance downgrade to the bridge where a guard was standing, and I planned to make it on foot if necessary. The driver climbed onto his seat, cracked his whip and started, and the guard stepped aside to let us pass. In the same moment, the stranger seemed to realize I was the one he was after. He rose from his seat to shout to the driver to stop.

Quick as a flash I drew my pistol, shoved its muzzle into his face, and commanded him to sit down. "If you open your head, I will blow it off!"

The women screamed, and as the startled driver heaved at the reins, I told him, "Drive across that bridge before I shoot you dead!"

I now had the whole bunch to contend with, and it kept me busy sitting on the ladies' laps trying to hold them down and keep my man and the driver in front of me. I soon had everybody silenced, except the women with their big hoop skirts floundering around. When we crossed the bridge, I made the detective get out and sent him high-tailing back to the States. The women declared I was crazy, the driver was in a flurry, but he was only too glad to drive to the end of his route and be rid of me. I had to stay at the line the rest of the night and wait for the next stage, but I was not molested. At 8 A.M., I took the stage for Magog, and my heart leaped with joy to know I was free at last.

When the town heaved in view, I was as excited as the day I killed my first bear and saved my old grandpa's life. It had changed a great deal—a good many new buildings had been put up—but everything else looked natural. I had changed a great deal too, for I had not been home in nearly four years, and when I got off the stage at the hotel, no one seemed to know me.

I went inside and stepped up to the register book. When I

scrawled my name across a whole page, old Winn, the manager, let out a big whoop and seized my hand warmly. He dashed up-stairs to the ballroom where the boys in Whitmore's Band were getting ready for a big dance, and down they came with several others, and such a greeting I never had. They asked a thousand questions, and after telling them how I had escaped my beastly doctor, they wanted to hear my full story and kept me talking a whole hour.

I went from the hotel to Thompson's Store and bought a fur muff for my mother. While I was there, a little boy came in, weighed himself on the scales, and went out. Mr. Thompson asked me: "Didn't you know who that was?"

I told him, "No."

He said, "Why, that is your youngest brother, Alphonso."

"It isn't possible!" I exclaimed, and ran after him. I hailed him at the bridge and asked: "Do you know who I am?"

He looked up at me and shook his head. Across the bridge we met Warren, and he did not know me either.

"Well," said I, "we will all go home together and let Mother decide."

As we entered the gate, my mother came rushing from the house. She threw her arms around me and wept. A loving mother always knows her own child. I met Father and my brother Albert in the kitchen, and they did not recognize me until I laughed. They could not believe I was home, and Father walked around sizing me up, like a man in a dream.

That evening we all went over to the church to the Christmas tree. It felt good to be with all my old friends again.

CHAPTER VII

Lincoln's Amnesty Proclamation and My Third Enlistment in 1865—The End of the Civil War—I Steal a Wife

Once more I was on the old roost, but there was a vacant chair that my grandfather used to occupy. Mother showed me the braid and button I had torn from my uniform in Buffalo that he so faithfully had delivered. The news spread quickly that Buckskin Joe was home again, and the Indians came out of the forest to see me. Even the old Indian Medicine Man was delighted. He still mourned the loss of my old grandpa whom he loved so well and trusted, and wanted me to go to the woods and live with him. But my father had started a hoop skirt factory in Magog. Hoop skirts were all the rage, and their manufacture had become a great enterprise. I went to work at the factory. A quiet life was more to my liking right now.

The fellow I had put off the stage at Derby Line, however, was not willing to forget that I was a deserter from the army. One day Albert boarded the steamboat *Mountain Maid* with a shipment of skirts going to the head of the lake at Newport, Vermont, and the detective arrested him, thinking he was me. The detective turned him loose when he discovered his mistake. Albert told me he was laying plans to kidnap me out of Canada, and after that, I went fixed for trouble.

In the summer of 1863, the Silver Brothers' Minstrels organized at Pidgeon Hill, in Missisquoi County, near the Vermont line, and

Jim Silver came after me to go on the road with them. The detective's determination to capture me had cooled some, but I took no chances. I signed up under the name of Ed Weaver, with the understanding that I was to make no appearances more than twenty miles over the Vermont and New York borders. The trip was a success, and I made some money.

That winter I joined the company of Eddy Knight, a jig dancer from Boston, who organized a show called The Parlour Circus. He was in the same fix as me, having deserted the army and fled to Canada. Our route was through the French country down the St. Lawrence River. It was a hard trip, a cold one, and we were always in the hole. We had to jump hotel bills as we beat our way from town to town. Sometimes we were forced to let our baggage out the window on ropes in the middle of the night, then go down on the ropes ourselves, and skip.

We had a performer named L. S. Sickles, who was a great contortionist. He would dislocate his joints and compress himself in a box sixteen inches square. One time, being hard pressed, I shipped him through in the box as baggage. Arriving in the night, the box was rolled onto the platform at the depot. Somehow the lock broke, and Sickles groaned and raised himself to full height in the moonlight. It was more than the freight handlers could stand. They fled to the baggage room, screaming and hollering, and gave Sickles the chance to quietly walk away.

We finally lost the poor fellow, though. He went over in New York to visit his relatives and got drafted into the army. Eddy and I headed north to Ottawa, where we disbanded the show and got jobs in a clothespin factory.

Here, in 1864, I saw Blondin No. 2 walk a rope across the big Kettle in the Ottawa River. [The "Kettle" was an immense whirlpool below Chaudiere Falls. The rapids began six miles above the city and ended at the falls, forty feet high. The river was navigable from its junction with the St. Lawrence to the falls and of considerable commercial importance because of the great quantity of fine timber cut on its banks and on those of its tributaries.] I had seen huge logs and even rafts go into that hole, and had been told that these logs, after disappearing, were next found in the ocean.

Blondin advertized that he would give $100 to anyone who had the nerve to let him carry him across the Kettle on his back. I thought it would be easy money, for the man seemed to know what he was doing. I approached him and announced that I was ready for the ride. "And," I added, "I'll sure stay with you—to the bottom of the Kettle, if necessary."

"Who are you that you dare to perform such a feat?" he asked.

"Oh," said I, "I'm just a fellow from the clothespin factory who needs that money pretty badly."

He whispered to me at once that he couldn't do it. "It was all talk—I wouldn't attempt such a thing."

I agreed to keep quiet and went away, for he was no fake. I saw him that night with torches on his balancing pole over the Kettle, and like a flash extinguish them and appear on the stage of the theater a mile away just a few minutes afterwards.

Eddy and I worked in the clothespin factory all winter and I planned to start a new show in the spring. Then President Lincoln issued his amnesty proclamation pardoning all deserters who reported themselves to a provost-marshal or returned to the regiments and companies to which they had been assigned within sixty days. We held a council of war to decide what to do. The proclamation was issued on March 11, so we had till May 10 to make up our minds.

At first, we thought about going back under the proclamation. I was due five months pay, and this seemed the only way to collect it. There was a hitch, however. We not only would have to serve the remainder of our original terms of enlistment but a period equal to the time lost by desertion, which we voted against. I came up with a better idea. There were a lot of people being drafted who were paying good money for substitutes. We could go back as somebody else and take a bounty. I felt that I had been robbed, and here was an opportunity to get even.

The latter part of March, we secured a small canoe and started across the St. Lawrence River to the States at the head of the

Lachine Rapids—the most daring attempt on water I ever made. In spite of all we could do, we were pulled into the rapids in the night. I made Eddy lay flat in the bottom of the boat, and the fight began. I headed the current and drifted as far as I dared. Then I turned the canoe and shot into the rapids at thirty miles an hour. If we could keep from being swamped in our pitching and diving, I was sure we would soon strike the opposite shore. Just before reaching the shore, we ran against a rock and smashed the side of the canoe. The next instant it was hurled into the air. I yelled for Eddy to jump, and we both jumped for our lives. We landed on the steep rock bank with the breath knocked out of us, and watched the boat disappear into the rapids.

We were not satisfied to be on land and commenced climbing the bluff to find a way out. It took us all night to find the road. Then we lit out for Ogdensburg, New York. After a good rest, we hunted up a recruiting agent for substitutes, who said he could get us $900 apiece if we could pass muster, and he thought we could.

He took us by train to Meadville, Pennsylvania, and there introduced us to the men we were to represent. They took us to the muster station where we were ordered to strip, jump, prance, and run down the hall. I cut loose with a few flip-flaps and started walking on my hands. That settled it. "He will pass," the officer said, and my man was so pleased he made me a present of a fine six-shooter.

Next came the description. In taking mine the officer was stuck, for I was tattooed more or less all over. "What do you call this, and what do you call that?" he asked.

I told him to call them whatever he liked, that I was now a soldier and not supposed to know anything. "In other words," said I, "I am supposed to be dead from here on."

Finally he turned to his clerk, and said, "Oh, put down a whole circus and menagerie. He will never go to the front anyway."

But I did, and it was nothing new to me. We were sent to Washington, thence to Richmond, Virginia, and assigned to the 98th Pennsylvania. I now took a good look at the war prison—

the one I had so narrowly escaped and where so many of our boys starved to death—and thought how less than three years before I had been picked up within six miles of the place in the Chickahominy swamps.

I also had a little fun. We were raw recuits, you know, and had to learn army tactics at once. During drill and the manual of arms, I made myself out so green and clownish that the drill sergeant himself had to laugh. I must have overdone it, for after we had broken ranks, he came around to get acquainted. He told me he believed I was qualified for anything in his line, that he was on to me, and that ended it.

On April 23, we were ordered on a forced march to Danville to assist in the capture of General Johnston's army. The second day out several of us got separated from the command and had to do a little foraging. About dark we came to a river. There was no bridge and we got a nigger to take us across in a boat. On the opposite bank we found some old shacks the Rebels had built for winter quarters and picked one to camp in for the night.

I asked the nigger if he knew where we could get some chickens and some applejack. He said he did, so I put him in front to lead the way. He took us through the woods to a big house. The nigger said, "Now, Massa's in the ash house an' de applejack's down in de ashes. And dis am de place."

I took Eddy with me and left the other boys with the nigger. I went to the front door and rapped hard. The door opened very slowly, and there stood an old man and woman and a wench. They seemed greatly surprised to see Yankees. "Don't be afraid," I said. "Have you any applejack to drink, or anything to eat?"

"No, suh, our boys done took everything we got," the old man replied.

"Well," said I, "we'll just stand here and visit while the boys have a look around."

Bang! went the ash house door, and soon the chickens begin to squawk. A pig ran across the lot, and Eddy stopped him with his bayonet. Then the other boys came up with a big keg of applejack.

"Old man," said I, "I thought you didn't have anything?"

He started trembling and begging us to spare their lives. I bid them goodnight, and we started back to camp with our lucky find. We had to stop several times to sample the applejack. The nigger refused to drink, and I soon found out why—by the time we reached camp, we didn't know whether we were afoot or horseback. We got so drunk we didn't wake up till the next morning. I went out to do some scouting and found where our command had passed in the night. We took after them, several hours in the rear, with what was left of the applejack in our canteens.

That evening we reached a little railroad station. The train was about to pull out with a load of supplies, so we boarded it in the dark, and along in the night discovered we were about to cross the river into Danville. I knew we had better get off, so I looked for an easy place to light. As the train started up a little grade, I gave the word, and we jumped. Such a tumbling and rolling of men, guns, knapsacks, haversacks, and canteens was a caution! Luckily, no one was hurt.

We struck out to hunt the main road, figuring to rejoin our command before it reached Danville, but soon came the order: "Halt! Who comes there?"

I said, "A friend without the countersign."

"Stragglers? Well, you can't go here."

So we had to steer off another direction. We made a wide circle, finally reaching the main road, and followed it to the bridge, where we were halted, arrested, and escorted into the city and placed in the bull pen. The next morning we were taken before the provost-marshal to give an account of ourselves. I explained that we had not been able to keep up and had fallen behind, that we had been doing our best to find our regiment, so he detailed a sergeant to escort us over to the 98th Pennsylvania. Our command had arrived at Danville on April 27—a little too late, for the day before, Johnston had surrendered his army to General Sherman in North Carolina.

As the boys were now in possession of Danville and needing some entertainment, they started a newspaper called the *Eolian* and opened a theater. In looking for talent, they settled on Eddy and me. "Another soft snap," said I, and we were back on the boards again. Hardly a night passed that I didn't see some of my old friends in the 49th New York, but fortunately, with my make-up on, none of them recognized me.

In a few days General Richard Taylor surrendered his Confederate forces in Mississippi and Alabama. About two weeks later, General Kirby Smith surrendered all the forces west of the Mississippi, and the war was over. Three cheers!

We received orders to march back to Washington. Since the war was over and we were on detached duty, Eddy and I decided to remain on the stage. We were immediately arrested, with many others, placed in the bull pen at City Point as prisoners of war, and guarded by nigger soldiers. We didn't like that very well. There was everything in the pen, all sorts and sizes from suckling calves to full grown elephants. But there was a little money in the crowd. So Eddy and I started a chuck-a-luck game, and soon had all the loose change.

As we had nothing else to do, everybody begin trying to figure a way to get out of the pen. I suggested that we tunnel under the wall to the magazine on the outside, blow it up, and all who survived could make their escape. We dug the tunnel, but just as we were ready to make our move, orders came for our release. We were put on a boat and taken to Washington. Eddy was among the first to be discharged. He bid me good-by and lit out for Boston, and I never heard from him afterwards.

It took me another two days to accomplish the act. I was handed a check, and at once presented it to the U.S. treasurer for cash. The cashier counted out that money faster than a hen picks up corn. I carefully counted it after him and discovered he had overpaid me $80, so I stepped back to the window, and asked, "Do you rectify your mistakes?"

"No, sir," he replied. "I do not make any."

"All right," I said, "I can stand it if you can," and walked out. I figured it was good pay for the time I had spent in the bull pen. I bought some citizens clothes and took the next train to Philadelphia.

I had planned to return to Canada, but ran into some boys from my old outfit who had been engaged by the Stone, Rosston, and Murray Circus, and they wanted me to go with them. [Den Stone, a clown and trick rider, had organized this show in partnership with Rosston about 1861. John H. Murray had joined it in 1864. It became the first show to tour the South after the war.] I sewed my money into the bottom of one of my pant legs, stuffed them inside my boots, then pawned my watch to the boss canvasman for $8. I now felt safe, for they all thought I was busted.

I was put to work on the seats. One day I remarked to my boss that I could jump around a little myself. He wanted to see what I could do, so I showed him a few tricks and some cross tumbling. He told the manager about me, and the manager asked if I would like to go into the ring. I told him I would like to go on the horizontal bar with the Denzer Brothers. One of them laughed at the idea, but when we were through, the laugh was on the other side. I was engaged as an acrobat.

I didn't stay with the show long. I couldn't stand the pressure on my leg. That poultice of greenbacks was drawing things to a head. I had to get rid of it some way. When we reached Jersey City, I settled up, redeemed my watch, and jumped the whole shooting match. I crossed the river into New York City and went up into New Hampshire to visit my old friend Whittier of the 3rd Vermont. I had not seen him since the siege at Yorktown and Young's Mills. He still had some money, so we set out to celebrate our army career and liberty.

Many things happened now that I cannot mention. We boarded the stage and rode all over the country. I remember we had a couple of dice we would throw to see who paid the bills. One night we got to feeling pretty good and took over a French hotel, and came near ending up in jail. Suffice it to say, we wound up in Canada under old Mt. Orford, where some of Whittier's folks lived, and I went home to Magog and another great reception. That fall I went trapping and hunting with the Indians on my old grandpa's stamping grounds, then drifted into silk smuggling. I paid seventy-five cents for the silk in Canada and got $4 a yard for it in the States. The law compelled the authorities to find the goods in my possession and they could not stop me as long as I was moving. I was on the move most of the time. But the business was too risky. The winter of 1865 I delivered my last roll of silk at Haverhill, New Hampshire, and went to visit Mrs. Russell Hutchins and her daughter Belle, who had been our neighbors in Canada. Mr. Hutchins, a soldier in the 3rd Vermont, had his leg shot off in May, 1863, at the Battle of the Wilderness. He lay on the field three days before he was picked up. By that time, mortification had set in, and he died in a hospital in Washington.

I already had proposed to Belle, and she had accepted. Her mother had not been favorable to the move, thinking her daughter too young at the time and that I was a little too wild. She would not change her mind now. The only thing to do was plan how to get away with my prize. Belle was employed as a nurse at a little place near Haverhill. Her trunk and clothes were there. I rented a livery rig and offered to drive her back to work.

Mrs. Hutchins could see nothing wrong with that. In fact, she thought it very kind of me. We bid her good-by, and it was the last time Belle ever saw her mother.

We picked up Belle's clothes and trunk. She told her employer that she was going with me to visit her sisters in Canada. So we drove to the railroad station, eight miles, and sent the team back to Haverhill. Then we took the train to Dunlap, got married, and went to North Enfield to the home of my old friend, Tom Watts.

CHAPTER VIII

Five Years on the Stage and in the Circus Ring, 1866 to 1870—Death of My Brother Warren

We took board with Tom and his wife at North Enfield, and I engaged to play the cornet in Blaisdell's Quadrille Band. Darkness clamped down with the winter sunset, and with primitive lighting and coal so costly, most folks banked their fires and were warm in their feather beds by nine o'clock. But on Saturday nights, there was always a community supper and a big dance.

From seven o'clock on, figures could be seen scurrying through the snow to the hall where the grand march opened promptly at eight. Waltzes, two-steps, and the quadrille were the vogue. These were often interrupted with special stunts by prize-seeking groups. Cash prizes were awarded the best costumed couple, comic, or unique performance. Supper was served during an hour's intermission at eleven, and by that time, the dancers were ready to traipse up the street to take their turn at the table. Then the dancing was resumed, the affair breaking up about two o'clock. The good times we had there I will always remember.

In the spring of 1866, I joined Yankee Annon's Comic Opera Troope, taking Belle with me. We traveled down to Massachusetts and Connecticut, then up through New York state, and did good business, closing in the fall at Gouverneur.

Yankee Annon was a typical Uncle Sam, and his wife, Sis, as we called her, was a genius and a great dancer. Our show consisted of tricks in legerdemain and exhibitions of herculean strength, together with instrumental and vocal music, comic songs, etc. [According to one contemporary account, "For ways that are dark and tricks that are vain, Professor Hoyt had no superior. His instrumental music was first class and never excelled in this place."] Besides all-around work, I did a speciality act under the title of a young foreign giant called "Iron Boy." This consisted of feats in light and heavy balancing, and permitting a solid stone of 400-pound weight to be broken upon my chest with a 14-pound sledge hammer in the hands of a bystander while I occupied a position elevated from the stage and supported merely at head and feet by chairs.

I had a 71-pound weight I used to curl my fingers around and hold out at arm's length in one hand. Yank always offered $500 to anyone who could handle and lift my weights as I did. Every night the strong men of the country would show up to try. One fellow put up $30 forfeit that he could beat me, and appeared for the contest. I went into a field and picked out a round boulder which I strapped in my sling for the occasion. I handled all my lighter weights first, then announced that I would handle and hold out the heavy boulder in one hand. I picked it up, shoving it to arm's length above my head, then with my arm straight, lowered it to a horizontal position, stopped it, then curled it to the floor to the starting point. The judges weighed the rock and gave it out as 78 pounds. A shout went up for my opponent to duplicate the feat, but he could not be found. [The newspaper account concluded: "Mr. Hoyt was the hero of the evening and he elicited frequent applause from the audience. Everybody appeared well pleased and hoped to see the Professor and his troop again."]

After the show disbanded at Gouverneur, Belle and I went to a little town called Silver, where the Silver Brothers lived, and I spent a few weeks trapping. Then the Dick Silver family and my wife and I started for the West, parting at Chicago, they going to Wisconsin, and Belle and I to Bloomington, Illinois, then out to Prairie City, in McDonough County, where my Uncle Charley Hoyt and Aunt Lucy lived. We took board with them that winter, and I learned the blacksmith trade. In the spring of 1867, Belle and I moved into my uncle's cane mill and set up housekeeping, our first home.

That summer a circus came to Bushnell, nine miles away, and we all went to see it, to be sure. I got to feeling pretty good and got into a little mix-up and knocked a man down. The Chief of Police told me if I would leave town, he would let me off. With some persuasion from my wife, I piled into the wagon and away we went for home. Uncle Charley soon overtook us in his two-wheeled trotting gig, so I switched over and rode with him. He was feeling pretty good himself, and we now hit a three-minute gait, sometimes in the ditch, sometimes in the road, but we got home right side up just the same.

In the fall a trainer came up to see me about running in a big foot race to be held at Macomb, the county seat. The best I could do on the first test was 100 yards in 16 seconds. I was discouraged, but he thought I had it in me to win. He put me in training, wearing weights on my feet. In thirty days, I was making 100 yards in 10 seconds, only a half second more than the record in those days. Well, I ran half a mile every morning behind a trotting horse on the track, and competed in the race against nine Indians and a white man. The white man would have won if he hadn't overheated himself. I managed to outdistance the Indians only by a fraction, capturing the big money, and became a favorite.

It was too cold that winter to keep house in the cane mill, so I got some rooms from a man named Turner for Belle and myself and my brother Warren, who had come out for a visit. J. T. Johnson's United Circus was wintering and playing in a large amphitheater at Macomb, and Warren and I engaged to perform for him. We worked hard three months, originating a good many acrobatic tricks. Johnson always boarded his performers, but one day toward spring, as we sat at the table, he said, "Eat hearty, boys, for this is your last meal." He thought he had us as a sure thing for the season and could save money by making us board ourselves.

On March 5, 1868, my wife gave birth to our first child, Ella. It was tough going for three days, dashing back and forth between the show and home in rain and snow and mud a foot deep, until our little daughter appeared on the great stage of life and the siege was over. Belle and the baby were in the good hands and home of the Turners. But Johnson had cut off our grub.

I immediately wrote the manager of the Great Western Circus at Albia, Iowa, for a job. My answer came at once, and on the first of April, Warren and I joined the Great Western at Albia, taking the road April 27. This was a wagon circus and a muddy season people read about. It was a first-class show and under good management, with Charley Fowler and Jim Smith as clowns; Joe Keys, two- and four-horse rider; the Chilean Acrobat; Warren and myself as the Canadian Brothers; and many other star performers of the day.

My brother was a very powerful and active man. Nobody had any business fooling with him. One day I saw him make our boss canvasman take a back seat pretty quick. Another time, Cramer, our manager, bet his landlord that he had a man who could take a pair of heavy pig irons, one in each hand, from a pile that was corded diagonally across the square from the hotel, carry them to the hotel steps, and lay them down without dropping them. The landlord covered the bet at once, with the remark: "Many have tried it, and nobody has done it yet."

Cramer called on my brother and told him what he wanted him to do. Warren walked over, picked up a couple of irons he could get a good grip on, and started. Fifty feet from the hotel, he started sinking. Old Cramer got excited, and pounding on the steps with his plug hat, hollered: "Lay them down here! Lay them down here!"

Warren laid them down all right. Cramer had ruined a $7 hat, but he won enough to buy a new one. At Aurora, Illinois, he won another bet when my brother lifted a shaft of iron weighing 1400 pounds square up from the ground with his hands. His heft was 180 pounds.

We left the show at Aurora on June 24, Warren going home to

Canada, and I going home to my wife and baby. After a week's visit, I joined Johnson's United Circus for a 4th of July celebration at Ridgely, and at Bement, September 17, on a wager, I turned the first double somersault on record. Old Johnson was only too happy to board me again, and I was heavily advertized as the first and only man in the world who ever turned twice in the air before landing after leaving the leaping board. I closed with his circus at Galesburg, Illinois, October 22, and went home to my wife and baby again.

My father and mother came out to see us, and we all moved to Bloomington for the winter, setting up housekeeping on West Washington Street. Warren came back from Canada and went to work in the coal mines, and I engaged to play in the local orchestra.

In the spring of 1869, we joined the George W. DeHaven Circus which was reorganized there. [DeHaven had operated a circus from 1861 to 1865, when control was acquired by Andrew Haight. Haight operated the show as the Haight & Chambers Circus in 1866, but lost heavily, and did not return to the business until 1871.] This was a railroad and steamboat circus. We started April 19 at Bloomington for a six-day stand. On May 5, we chartered a steamboat at St. Louis and went up the Mississippi to St. Paul, Minnesota, showing in every town on each side of the river, thirty in all, arriving at St. Paul on June 10.

We had a fat woman with the sideshow named Tom Hose. She weighed 400 pounds. At Dubuque, Iowa, she was taken sick, and right after the evening performance, I returned to the boat and seated myself near her stateroom door to write a letter. I was so impressed something was wrong that I silently opened the door just enough for a squint inside and discovered she was dead. I gave the alarm, and the undertaker had to hurry for she had been dead several hours and was bloating fast. They finally got a coffin big enough by six men standing on the lid to screw it down, and got her in the ground just in time to save an explosion.

After leaving Dubuque, a large floating palace with a dance hall and all kinds of amusements followed us, taking advantage of the crowds we drew. Two nights of this was all we could stomach

85

The next night Warren and I and the Austin Brothers boarded the palace and made a clean sweep by tossing its managers and all its paraphernalia into the river. It was fun for the boys, and the boat didn't follow us any more.

We played Minneapolis on June 12, crossed the river at St. Anthony above the falls, then took the railroad back south through Iowa. In the town of Cresco, my brother received a fatal blow, leaping.

I was in charge of the act. We always wound up with him making the leap for life and I doing a double somersault over the backs of running horses. We were using a running board for the first time, and it was difficult to keep from overthrowing. We had reached twelve horses abreast and it was Warren's turn to go. I saw him hesitate, and motioned him on. He leaped, jumping everything in front of him, but overthrowed on the second turn and landed on his chest in the bank of the clay ring.

As he walked past me to the dressing room, I could see he wasn't breathing. I hurried through my double and when I reached the room he was just getting his breath. He thought he was going to be all right, but I was afraid and sent him home to be doctored. I went on with the show, and on Saturday, July 3, at Whitewater, Wisconsin, as I sat my horse ready for the grand entry, a boy rushed up and handed me a telegram. It read: "Come quick. Warren is dying."

I was so dazed my entry was almost a failure. I took the train that evening for Chicago, arriving in Bloomington at noon Monday, but too late. Warren had passed away on the 3rd and was buried on Sunday, my mother's birthday. I went to the cemetery and turned a backward somersault over his grave. This was the custom of all acrobats of the time.

I thought then of giving up circus life, but I was under contract for the season. I rejoined my company on the 16th at Green Bay, Wisconsin, and we were routed through Illinois and Indiana to Cincinnati, Ohio, arriving there September 16 for a four-day stand, where I contested with Kelly and Rhinehart [professional acrobats] doing doubles. They had now learned my trick.

86

But I out-did them by doing a perfect thribble—I turned over three times and landed straight on my feet after leaving the board. It was my science to always light standing, which Kelly and Rhinehart could never do. They would hold to their trick until landing then bob up—what I called a "prat-double." I had perfected the art, and they acknowledged that they could not beat me.

The management changed hands here to Mike Lipman, who wound up in a lawsuit with the railroad company at Harper's Ferry, Virginia. When I learned they were attaching the show, I slipped my pye box and baggage out in the night and shipped everything home, arriving in Bloomington myself on October 25. I had traveled through eleven states in all. The circus had traveled exactly 6,528 miles, and I had turned exactly 6,528 somersaults.

Still unwilling to give up the life, I engaged to go with the Metropolitan Circus in 1870. I joined my company at Crawfordsville, Indiana, April 12. This was a railroad circus, but we changed to a wagon show the middle of July, and ended the season October 15 at Louisville, Kentucky. The Watson Brothers and myself were then engaged to play in Lout's Iron Building, New York City, for the winter, under a $500 challenge as bar performers, and on the strength of this, I sent my family to my old home in Canada.

In a short time my wife gave birth to our second child, another girl we named Clara Mabel, and since there was no chance of having my family in New York City for the winter, I cancelled my engagement with the Watson Brothers and decided I was through with my circus career.

Looking back now at its trials and tribulations, I must say it was a dog's life. You pulled out at all hours from midnight to 4 in the morning, and tried to rest and sleep while being hauled in a jolting wagon over all kinds of roads and in all kinds of weather. You arrived at the next town between 6 and 8 o'clock, ate breakfast, then hurried down to the dressing room to overhaul your wardrobe, do a little mending, and wash out a suit of tights, and got ready for the parade. After the parade, you rushed through dinner and got ready for the afternoon show. It took all the energy and force you could muster to do your work in the ring. As soon as the afternoon show was over, you hurried through supper and back to the tent for the night performance. After the night show, you packed, took your berth in the hack, and hung on like grim death to keep from being thrown out in another five-hour-long drive to the next stand. Still no sleep or rest. You kept this up for six months and wondered how you stayed in condition to do such artistic work. You went into the ring with that artificial smile and those bewitching gestures and poses, and heard such remarks as, "Oh, ain't he nice. How good he must feel. What a fine life actors must have. Golly, wish I was an actor too." I often thought, *one peep behind scenes would sure change their notion*!

On top of all these luxuries came the congestive chills and fever like I had one season down in Little Egypt on the Wabash and at Evansville on the Ohio River. I have lost count of the times the manager had to rub my back with Wizard Oil and give me a half pint of whiskey before I could get down to the tent to do my work.

And there were the two hard fights we had with bushwhackers in the South. One night we had to pack and leave town without a performance. Our boss canvasman caught three fellows trying to cut the ropes on our main tent and killed them with a toe pin and threw their bodies in a well.

But I am compensated with fond memories of the fine performers I worked with: Jim Smith, Charley Fowler, John Foster, and Jimmy Reynolds, clowns; great riders like Barney Carroll, Ben McKinley, Joe Keys, Edith Johnson, and John Robinson; tightrope dancers, Madam Bridges and Ena Eddy; Beswick, the Chilean Acrobat; Arabs Hashino and Hashamalie; acrobats like the Denzer Brothers, Miller Brothers, Austin Brothers, Castle Brothers, Watson Brothers, the Reynolds family, Kelly and Rhinehart, Tom Peppers, and many others too numerous to mention.

Tom Peppers, "Old Pep" we used to call him, was the only tramp acrobat I ever knew. He never engaged to any company, he belonged to them all. I have seen him, after walking forty miles, come into our dressing room whistling and, with a "Hello, boys," hunt up a suit of tights that would fit him, always without asking, and go into his tumbling act. He was the greatest low tumbler in the world. He was a privileged character and took his spirits where he found them. We always locked our pye boxes when we saw him coming. I once saw him jump off a bridge into the river with his clothes on in zero weather for a pint of whiskey.

Which brings to mind a young man named Porter who visited our circus in Iowa. He was the only survivor of the Porter family, massacred by the Sioux in Minnesota in 1862, and had just got out of the hospital after several bullets were extracted from his body. He had knelt on the ashes of his home and sworn to kill 100 Indians to avenge his people's death. He showed me a small stick he carried with 80 notches cut on it, indicating the number he had killed already, and told me he was then on his way to complete his task. I traded hats with him for luck. He agreed to write me how he came out, but never did. I have often wondered if he reached the 100-mark.

CHAPTER IX

Off to a Life in the Far West—Southern Kansas and Indian Territory in the '70's, Scouting and Fighting Indians

As I now had another mouth to feed and had quit the circus life, my brother Albert proposed that I go with him to the Western frontier. He had spent two months in Iowa and Illinois, buying and cribbing corn, and come back with some money and glowing tales of opportunities in Kansas. [The Homestead Law of 1862 provided that a man who was the head of a family, twenty-one years of age, and a citizen of the United States, or had declared his intention to become such, could acquire 160 acres of public land for a moderate fee on condition of cultivation and occupancy as a home for a period of five years. The time that any settler had served in the army or navy could be deducted. The liberal provisions of the law had attracted thousands of settlers to Kansas from the eastern and central states. Most of them were Union men who had gone there each year since the Civil War. Many were foreigners newly arrived in America. Nearly all of them were poor, with scarcely enough to provide for themselves until harvesting their first crop. But they were full of hope and willing to undertake the toil and privations to make their dreams come true. They were turning the bare plains into fertile fields. Pioneer homes dotted the eastern part of the state more thickly, and the line of settlement was moving rapidly westward and south to Indian Territory.] I decided to take up a border life once more, wild and woolly, and fitted out at once for the trip. This move caused a great change in my career.

We secured tickets to Topeka, and upon our arrival found that we could get as far south as Emporia on the Santa Fe, so we went down on one of the first passenger trains and stopped a few days to look things over. It soon got out that Buckskin Joe, the famed acrobat, was in town, and my brother tried to change my name to "Buffalo" Joe. The buffalo business never stuck, but the fun commenced. We attended the dances and I got to cutting up and playing the fiddle. This was quite a lively place at the end of the railroad.

A fellow named Vandorn had made up a party for the extreme southern border and the Arkansas River, and asked us to join them. This party consisted of several families with two horse teams and one ox team belonging to a man named Whitney, whose wife had a nursing babe. I scouted out the country ahead, hunting crossings and making camps, and kept all well supplied with wild game, which was plentiful. The streams and steep banks were bad to cross, but we pulled through in good shape, landing in Cowley County the latter part of November, 1870, on a high stretch of prairie between the Arkansas and Walnut, at a little trading post called Creswell, now Arkansas City. The wolves were so thick we had to stand guard at night for safety. West of the Arkansas, buffalo still could be counted by the thousands, about four miles south was the Indian Territory border, and the camps of Osage Indians were all around us. I threw my hat in the air, and shouted, "Eureka!" I was back in the wilds again and, to be sure, in my glory.

The little trading post wasn't a year old yet, but the town had been laid out and every week or so other settlers would join us. A good many already had staked claims around the town. [During the summer of 1869, the Endicott brothers, Pat and E. C., and their party had taken up residence along the rivers near the post. On the first of January, 1870, John Brown, John Strain, T. A. Wilkinson, and G. H. Norton claimed the four quarter sections on which the town now stands, and called the settlement Walnut

City. A little later it was called Creswell, and still later, Arkansas City. Norton erected the first house on the site, but other huts had been constructed along the rivers by the members of the Endicott party. Norton's log house served as the first store and post office. In April, 1870, he had been appointed postmaster. On June 10, Judge W. P. Campbell of the 13th judicial district had issued the order for incorporation.] My friend Whitney crossed the Walnut on the east with his wife and baby and erected a little shack of brush and rock under a big bluff to live in the rest of the winter. Vandorn and the others located around the land we camped on, and I squatted on a claim two miles northwest in a jackoak grove where I could hunt and trap on the Arkansas. Nevertheless, we were on Osage lands, and the Indians did not understand why we were laying claim to their country. They did not like it much either, and begin to show in their actions.

[Cowley County, the fifth county west of Missouri on the Indian Territory border, had been carved from the diminished reserve of the Osage Indians, a section which had been a source of contention since 1868. For many years prior to the opening of the Kansas territory to settlement, it had been the government's policy, in treating with the Indians in the more settled sections of the country, to give them the privilege of selecting reservations in the uninhabited portions of the West. A number of the tribes were induced to cross the Missouri and make their homes in Kansas, a land of genial climate and undulating surface capable of producing maize with very little labor, where the buffalo roamed in countless herds, and deer, wild turkey, prairie chicken, and quail were always within reach of the hunter's arrow. Among these immigrant tribes were the Iowas, Kickapoos, Delawares, Pottawatomies, Sacs and Foxes, Ottawas, Shawnees, Wyandottes, and Miamis. Their reservations embraced the choicest portions of the territory and were carved out of the domain which the government acquired by purchase from the Osage and the Kansas, or Kaw, Indians, at the same time leaving large areas to the Osages and the Kaws. On the admission of the state to the Union in January, 1861, nearly all Indian reservations within the state's limits were surrounded by white settlers. The necessity arose for further negotiations, and the Indians, tribe after tribe, moved south to reservations in Indian Territory. Among the last to part with their lands were the Osages. Their diminished reserve, far exceeding any other Indian reservation in Kansas, extended 50 miles north and south to the Indian Territory border, and from the present west boundary of Crawford and Cherokee counties, 260 miles west, embracing 1,300 square miles, or 9,300,000 acres.

[In May, 1868, the Osages met with government officials on Drum Creek, below Humbolt. The result was the notorious Sturgis treaty, which emphasized the settlers' grievances that Indian land, instead of becoming public domain, was passing to corporations. N. G. Taylor, the Indian commissioner sent out from Washington, had allowed William Sturgis, president of the Leavenworth, Lawrence & Galveston Railway of Chicago, to be the controlling spirit, inducing the Osages to cede to the United States for resale to the railroad their entire reserve for an average price of twenty cents per acre. Prior to Kansas statehood, it had been the policy of the government to purchase the reservations outright, the reservations thus reverting directly to the United States and the law governing public lands. Later, companies and combinations, by urging their measures day and night in the lobbies of Congress, ostensibly in behalf of public interests, but actually through motives of personal gain, managed to secure for themselves, and on their own terms, nearly all the reservations and trust lands in the state.

[As soon as the settlers heard the provisions of the treaty, they took active steps to defeat its ratification. The Honorable Sidney Clarke, congressional representative of the southeast Kansas district, was flooded with petitions; the attorney general of Kansas, pressed by the incensed state officials, hurried off to Washington; and the Osages, now seeing that it was an attempt to rob them, added their protest. Congressman Clarke espoused the cause of the settlers and the Indians and exposed the fraud in the House so forcibly that the Senate was obliged to reject the treaty. Nearly a year later, after a number of defeats, he succeeded in obtaining the passage of a joint resolution opening the lands to settlement. But there were powerful forces just as determined to recognize the railroad claim. They not only defeated Clarke when he came up for re-nomination for Congress, but also succeeded in having the railroad's case argued before the Department of the Interior. Secretary Delano decided in favor of the corporation. Several local suits were then instituted by the settlers, but were withdrawn because the litigants decided to seek relief in the federal courts. The impression prevailed, however, that the United States had no jurisdiction because the land had been conveyed by treaty; so the Kansas legislature petitioned Congress to pass a law giving the federal government jurisdiction.

[Meanwhile, the settlers were trespassing on Indian land. The Indians were numerous, and realizing the insecurity of the whites in the county, began to steal and make unfriendly demonstrations.] That winter, about a hundred redskins surrounded the Thomas boys' cabin ten miles above my camp and built fires around the place, giving a war dance. We got the message in the night, and I set out with a dozen good men and plenty ammunition, arriving just in time, for they already had set fire to the house to get the boys outside to scalp them. When we opened a fusillade on them, they gave out with hideous yells, mounted their ponies, and lit out. By the blood on the ground, I could tell they had packed a few away badly hurt. The boys were mighty thankful to get out alive, and they moved down closer to the settlement.

This action about put a stop to immigration in the county, and we looked for a general uprising at any time. I came in from running my traps one evening to learn that a small band had been skulking back of my place in the grove. I owned a buckskin pony and mounted at once, scouting the country to the north. I soon located them on my spring branch a half-mile away.

Indians had never been a source of torment to me. The Osages seemed no more warlike than my Canadian friends. They were fine specimens, and I had great admiration for them. Like all Indians, they admired bravery. I rode up to them and told their old chief, No-po-wa-lee, in sign language to be gone at sunrise or

95

I would open fire on them. I was up and on my buckskin at daybreak, fixed for execution. They were still on the branch, so I lit out for them and commenced shooting at long range. They mounted their ponies, and all I could see was the streak of dust they left behind. I nearly fell off my horse, laughing.

No-po-wa-lee came to see me several times after that. I had a red circus entry jacket covered with silver spangles, and he was delighted with it. It was too small for him, but he would always try it on. He offered me six buffalo robes for it, but that was no inducement. I told him I could go west and kill buffalo and get all the robes I wanted any day. I finally gave him the jacket to keep him away from camp.

But that didn't stop him. One day right after I had finished my dugout, the old chief showed up. He couldn't see anything but smoke coming out of the ground. His curiosity was aroused and he commenced circling the smoke like a wild goose or antelope. Suddenly I poked my head out of the earth. The old Indian gave one big grunt and a jump, but seeing my buckskin clothes, recognized me at once and approached with a "How, how, Joe Buck."

I invited him inside, thinking to have a little fun. I stirred up the fire, and when the smoke begin to get thick, I told him to stay in the dugout and I would get him something to eat. Outside, I covered the chimney with a deer skin. The old man stood it as long as he possibly could, for all the time I was making more smoke instead of looking for grub. All at once I heard a big whoop, and out he came, and off he went into the woods, never to return.

The land fuss was finally settled in Washington. Congress fixed it so the Osages sold their land to the United States, the settlers got it at $1.25 per acre, and the proceeds were used to buy the Osages enough land for a reservation in Indian Territory. [This tract consisted of 1,700,000 acres lying west of the ninety-sixth meridian, bounded on the north by the southern border of Kansas, on the west and south by the Arkansas River, and was the extreme eastern part of the old Cherokee Outlet to which the government laid claim in the 1866 treaties after the Civil War. The Osages also agreed to assign a part of their domain to the Kaw Indians as a home, and 100,000 acres in the northwestern corner was reserved for the Kaws.] The Indians started moving to their new reservation in 1871, the settlers started pouring in, and the government surveyors started laying off the country in quarter sections.

This caused us squatters a good deal of trouble. In many cases, the survey lines left two on one claim and a contest was on at once to see who had the prior right. We couldn't straddle lines. The government insisted that we conform to squares. In my case one man shoved his neighbor into the Arkansas River, and in doing so, abandoned an eighty on the north, which left a full quarter section for someone, and his own brother advised me to squat on it, so I did. Then it was declared we could straddle lines, his neighbor drove him back on the south, and the man tried to shove me off. I objected, and he became profane about it.

"Well," I said, "I know a quick way to bury the hatchet." He wanted to know my proposition, so I told him, "Lay down your arms and I'll lay down mine. We'll meet in the middle of the prairie with bare fists. The best man wins."

He was a big fellow, well-muscled, and I could tell he thought he had me bested. He nodded, and said, "That should end it for all time."

We unbuckled our knives and six-shooters, grounded them beside our rifles, and advanced to the center. He made the first pass, and missed. I feinted with my right, and he leaped back, leaving just room enough for my jump. I struck him in the face with both feet. He sprawled backwards, flat on the grass, and lay there, his face badly cut and bleeding.

I invited him to get up, and said, "I will not take the advantage when you are down. If you care to try again, I will be here."

Up he came in a mad rush swinging with great force. I dodged the blow and hit him in the side of the neck as he went past, downing him the second time and this time disabling him so that he was willing to give up. We shook hands and closed the deal. I mention this merely to show how easy it was to settle disputes without courts, lawyers, or money.

The first sawmill was set in operation on the Arkansas by William Sleath and Son. Early in 1871, a second one was started on the Walnut by the Spears brothers. The timber belts along the streams varied from a quarter to a half mile in width and contained cottonwood, elm, hackberry, mulberry, walnut, oak, redbud, pecan, hickory, ash, and cedar. I bought cottonwood lumber, about the first that was sawed, to build a house.

It was built mathematically, for my brother figured out everything and I cut the lumber and put it together. As I was putting up the last rafter, an old fellow came along. He must have been a carpenter, for he squinted awhile, then called out, "You are out of plumb. The house leans to the south."

"Too late now," I shouted back. "It is all nailed."

"Are you going to leave it that way—out of line?" he asked.

"No," said I, "my brother will figure it back. How about it, Al?"

"Why sure," said Albert, "if I figured it out of line, why not figure it back?"

The old man shook his head and went on, but every little bit he would turn and stare at us. I suspect our method was new to him. My house was like the Dutchman's—it was not much for pretty, but it was hell for strong. The day we shingled it, the wild geese lit around us so thick we could kill them with rocks. They had no fear and seemed perfectly tame.

As I now had everything in readiness for a border life, I wrote my wife to come to the Far West and share with me. She came with the children over the long road from Canada, on the Santa Fe from Topeka to Cottonwood Falls [the railroad had reached this point during the winter], then by stage 120 miles, with many streams to ford and slippery, steep hills and banks to climb, arriving in Arkansas City the last of April, 1871. My neighbor, Yellowstone Steward, happened to be coming from town with a load of lumber and heard her inquiring for Buckskin Joe.

"Why," he said, "we practically live next to each other only two miles from here. You can ride right out to his door." And as I was standing in the doorway about 3 P.M., I saw Steward coming down the trail with his load of lumber all covered with luggage and people. I recognized my family at once and ran to greet them. The first thing I did, my wife said, was raise the veil of the baby and kiss her, and Ella, my oldest, hardly knew me.

In just fifteen minutes I made a cradle for the baby out of some scrap lumber and a bed for Ella out of my old circus trunk. Then my wife and I settled down to housekeeping. It was more like "house-camping," for we had no furniture. But we had great expectations and were bound to take things as they came, with "Live and Let Live" over the door.

We had a good deal to contend with at first. Flour and bacon were scarce items, and everything had to be hauled or freighted from Cottonwood Falls. I planted the first hedge on this border for a windbreak, set out one of the first orchards, and planted some of the first corn and wheat. It was hard to raise much to live on. The summer was hot, dry, and windy with frequent sand storms. When it rained it poured, with thunder and lightning and water spouts. The winter was one of the coldest ever. A few nights during a blizzard, I had to bring my buckskin pony and dog inside with the family, and was forced to take the hay out of our beds to feed the horse. The cottonwood house had shrunk so the cracks were about an inch wide, and the snow came in everywhere with the wind and cold—at 16 below zero. Water even froze in the teakettle on a hot stove.

But we fared well. I hunted and trapped on the Arkansas. When I wanted turkey or prairie chicken, all I had to do was walk up into the timber and kill them. I had a small English shotgun for chickens that I always kept in the house, and one day while I was running my traps, Belle thought she would try her hand shooting. The chickens were thick in the trees, for snow was on the ground.

Belle got the gun down, and failing to find a cap on the tube, supposed it was not loaded. So she loaded the gun, put on a pair of my boots, and struck out. The chickens wouldn't let her get close enough to shoot them, and finally she got tired walking in my boots and came back to the house. She was so mad and disgusted she had to shoot something. The lid from my old circus trunk was laying on the woodpile behind the house, so, standing in the back door, she pulled up the old gun and blazed away at the trunk lid. She hit it all right, but the gun flew out of her hands, bruising her face and knocking her down, and she was plumb deaf, for she told me she could see the children with their mouths open, crying, and could not hear a thing. My pony was running down in the corral with his tail up and snorting, and my dog hid out. The turkeys in the jackoaks went to gobbling and the chickens to cackling, and all flew for the tall timber in confusion. No wonder— with two loads in that gun! She never seemed to have any desire to hunt after that.

That same winter my brother and Bill Hackney [later mayor of Winfield], left my place with an ox team loaded with lumber and traveled 35 miles up the Arkansas, crossed the river near the mouth of Dog Creek, and laid out the town of Belle Plaine on the Cowskin. After the great blizzard came down from the north, I was up the Arkansas on a hunt and decided to visit their camp. I crossed the river on the ice and waded several miles through drifts, but no sign of life. It was by accident that I stumbled onto a chimney sticking out of the snow. When I sent out a warwhoop, they replied and dug a hole through to let me in. They had been snowed under two days, living on half rations, and were whittling up their last box to keep from freezing. I made for the timber and brought up some wood, and left what supplies I had to carry them through until they could pack in more fuel and provisions. I think this experience caused Albert to give up life on the unfriendly plain, for he soon left Kansas. Later, he and brother Alphonso engaged in the manufacturing business at Minneapolis, Minnesota.

These were times to try men's souls. Many of the pioneers gave up in despair, but most of them stayed, and because like attracts like, this brave, hardy race drew others who were determined to dominate for principle, and because they needed land for homes. In May, 1872, the railroad reached Wichita, and we got our supplies from there. Cowley County had 5,000 acres of wheat that year, which brought 80 cents a bushel, after being carted by ox and mule teams to the market at Wichita. Wichita was quite a town, handling most of the cattle trade of the southwest and having all the undesirable conditions connected with it. Arkansas City grew also. Our population jumped to 900, and people were still coming.

One day the stage rolled into town with a musician who had a few old brass horns. Steward located him on a claim north of mine, and we soon had a Buckskin Border Brass Band organized and going some. Besides myself, eleven recruits—John Breene, Peter Pearson, Edward Thompson, A. Wells, Charlie Balkum, T. Wilkinson, C. Burkey, Charlie Grimes, Herman Goddard, Yellowstone Steward, and D. D. Lewis—composed the noisy aggregation that caused the Indians to say, "Joe Buck makum heap big noise, heap scarum buffalo." We played for the first 4th of July celebration ever held in the city and every other important occasion. With this and my violin for dancing, I made more money than by farming.

Another way I made some money was killing buffalo. The old scout O. P. Johnson and I were great friends. Johnson had served with the army during the Indian wars of 1868 and 1869 in western Kansas and Indian Territory. We were together a great deal on the plains in 1873. Most of the hunting was being done by large organized outfits, who were better equipped to resist the Indians and the elements and the pressures against the wholesale slaughter of the buffalo. But Johnson and I went our own way. We got from one to two dollars a hide, and dressed out the meat and sold it to roadranches and to any hungry landseeker we met on the trails.

Then there were the wealthy ducks from the East who always wanted to go on a hunt so they could go back and tell about killing buffalo in company with the scouts. I remember two fellows came to Arkansas City that fall. We fitted out in good shape with plenty of everything, even good cigars and wine, and with a good salary. It was fine weather, and we determined to make the job interesting for a continuance. The second day out we spied an old bull lying quite natural down a long basin in a

101

wallow, and we laid out the route for them to make a sneak on him.

"Be sure to crawl low and not show yourselves," Johnson said. "If he raises to run, we'll be here to drive him back so you can have a chance to shoot him."

They lit out crawling on their bellies through mud and sand-burrs, and we rolled and laughed, took another drink of wine, and lit up twenty-five-cent cigars. Everytime they looked back, we would motion them on. When they had crawled close enough, we gave the signal to shoot, and you should have heard them open on the old fellow. They got so excited they commenced to advance, and kept shooting, and we laughed till our sides hurt. Then we went down to inspect their work. "Why, boys," I said, "you have killed him too dead to skin." They soon discovered he had been dead for a week, and a great laugh went up from all hands. But I don't think they appreciated the joke like we did.

They soon killed some live buffalos, however, and we took home the "fries" and had them served at the Wolsey Hotel. Everyone admired the dish, and one lady asked Johnson, "What part of the animal is that?" He hesitated and tread on my toes for an answer. "Why, madam," said I, "that is part of the lower kidneys." She never learned different, for when we were ready to leave on our next hunt, she came to the door and called to me, "Now, Joe, don't you forget to bring me some more of those lower kidneys."

That same year we built the first church in Arkansas City, by subscription, and named it the Liberal Church—open to all alike. We finally run out of money and I gave an entertainment and a ball in Pearson's Hall with the deacon at the door, donating the proceeds to aid in its completion, which took place on November 19. And the first talk ever made in this church was on temperance by a man who was drunk. No man could predict as he did, and all came true except the lie he told about seeing elephant tracks in the Indian country below us.

Which brings to mind the town drunk, Old Gutch. One winter night I came in from a long trip with my mustache and long hair all covered with frost and rode my buckskin into the main saloon. As I entered, I sang out at the top of my voice, "And Satan came also."

Old Gutch, who was a regular boarder at the place, tall, lanky and lean, rose from the rear of the room with the answer, "Yes, and a Jackass opened his mouth and spake."

A big laugh went up, and everybody ordered a drink. One man said, "Kinder got you that time, Joe."

"Yes," said I. "It don't need any argument." And I paid for the drinks all around.

Gutch was a witty fellow. One day he asked Elder Swarts, the oldest man in that country, if he would kindly answer a question from the Bible.

"Certainly, Mr. Gutchis. What is it?"

"You know," said Gutch, "where we read about the Golden Calf?"

"Yes, yes."

"Wal, c'n you tell me what sex that calf was, a bull or a heifer?"

Another time, he stepped into McMullin's bank for a loan. The banker thought he could do more good by giving him some advice. "Gutchis, why don't you quit drinking, save your money and have something in your old age to fall back on?"

Gutch indignantly remarked, "By gag, Mr. McMullin, I have something to fall back on in my old age."

"I am glad to hear it, Gutchis. What might it be?"

"The same thing Balaam fell back on."

CHAPTER X

The Indian War of 1874—Panic, Drought,
and the Grasshopper Plague—I Organize
the "Ragged-Ass Militia"

Arkansas City continued to grow. By 1874, we had a real live, permanently located boot-black. A man named Buzzie held the reputation of being the best stone mason in the country. We had three ministers and one lawyer, one brass band and two string bands, and our teams beat all comers at croquet and chess games. Christian Harader, a member of the old Dunkard sect which believed in full beards for men, set up a little red mill on the Walnut northeast of town. He was a preacher, one of a sizable colony of the order living in that vicinity. I reckon he never shaved in his life, but he did good business grinding grist for the settlers and Indians. One month over 60,000 pounds of freight was delivered at the Osage Indian Agency from Arkansas City by four- and six-horse and mule teams. We even had high hopes of becoming an inland "seaport." The first steamer to navigate the Arkansas this far north made its landing, and I marched through the street with my Buckskin Band, boarded her, and played a concert on her deck. Her name was *Aunt Sally*. Another boat named the *Kansas Miller* made regular trips between Arkansas City and Fort Smith, Arkansas, for some time, taking flour down the river and bringing back other freight, as well as excursionists.

But all wasn't as rosy as appeared. The fiery summer winds and heat of three years had dried up everything. There was no

105

stench even from a dead carcass, and like the Indians, we would jerk our meat and hang it up in the sun to cure for future use. Our newspaper, the *Traveler*, published an official statement that there were 4,000,213 acres of land under cultivation in Kansas, and that was the trouble. As soon as we commenced to plow the soil and dying vegetation took place, the chills and fever followed, and the tall grass made its appearance and ran out all the buffalo grass, and the white man ruined the country for the wild Indians.

The Indians had to give way to the high-grade, progressive, intelligent white man, a land of the free, land of fine churches and 40,000 licensed saloons, forts and guns, houses of prostitution, millionaires and paupers, theologians and thieves, Christians and chain gangs, trusts and tramps, money and mimicry, virtue and vice; a land where you can get a bad drink for five cents and preachers are paid $25,000 a year to dodge the devil and tickle the ears of the wealthy, where we have a congress of 400 men to make laws and a supreme court of nine to set them aside, where men vote for what they do not want for fear they will not get what they do want by voting for it, where niggers can vote and women cannot, where to be virtuous is to be lonesome and to be honest is to be a crank, where we sit on the safety valve of energy and pull wide open the throttle of conscience, where gold is the one thing sought after, where we teach the Indian eternal life from the Bible and kill him off with bad whiskey, where we put a man in jail for stealing a loaf of bread and in Congress for stealing a railroad, where corruption permeates our whole social and political fabric and we have the greatest aggregation of good things and bad things, hot things and cold things, all sorts and sizes, ever exhibited in any so-called civilized country on the globe.

The Indians begin to show a realization of what was coming and a disposition to go on the warpath. [By the terms of the Medicine Lodge Treaty, the country south of the Arkansas was reserved from settlement and regarded as the exclusive hunting ground of the tribes of the Southern Plains. When the treaty was made, in 1867, buffalo were still numbered by the million, and the white hunters confined most of their killing to the north side of the river. Then the Atchison, Topeka and Santa Fe Railroad was built up the valley of the Arkansas through Western Kansas. It reached Dodge City in 1872. In 1873, it was extended to Granada, Colorado. By this time buffalo north of the river had become scarce, and many hunters began to slip across on the south side. Government troops patrolled the river at intervals as a feeble indication that the treaty had not been forgotten, but the hunters had no difficulty crossing back and forth without detection. By 1874, they had extended their operations into the Texas panhandle. Texas, when admitted to the Union, had reserved all public land, and not having been consulted in the treaty, the state made no effort to prevent this invasion. To expedite the work of the hunters, several parties from Dodge City had planted a trading settlement near the mouth of a small tributary of the South Canadian in the heart of the southern buffalo range—at Adobe Walls. From this point, large numbers of hunters had scattered over the surrounding country, and the Cheyennes, smarting under these violations and faced with starvation or a change in their way of life with the extermination of the buffalo, made strong efforts to induce all the tribes to join in a general uprising. Many of the tribes refused, but most of the Comanches and some of the Kiowas joined them, and launched the Indian War of 1874.] The Kansas press warned the border settlements to be on the lookout for war parties. The *Traveler* suggested, "It will be best to go in large parties this fall and keep together when hunting, or someone will come back baldheaded."

This was after Tom Baird returned from Indian Territory to get help to search for some missing surveyors. Baird was a member of a military escort sent out in the spring with a 25-man crew to set lines over the section. Six of the surveyors, working away from the company, had disappeared on the Cimarron. We found five of them in one place. They had been killed and scalped and their bodies mutilated. We buried them close to the spot where they lay, and the body of the other man, Ed Deming, found later, was brought back and buried at Arkansas City. These killings were supposed to have been done by Cheyennes.

At dawn, on June 27, 700 Comanches, Kiowas, and Cheyennes attacked 28 white men and one woman at Adobe Walls. About 2 o'clock in the morning, the weight of the heavy dirt roof on one of the buildings had cracked the big cottonwood ridgepole that supported it. If some of the men had not been up repairing the roof, all would have been surprised and killed while asleep. The buffalo hunters were expert marksmen and their long range rifles cut down the ranks of the charging redskins. They stood them off two days until other hunters got word of the attack and started arriving from the plains, and the Indians retreated. They carried away most of their dead and wounded, leaving about a dozen dead warriors who were so close to the buildings that it would have been suicide to have tried to remove them. There were about 60 dead horses.

[This brief account was hearsay with Hoyt and therefore not entirely accurate. For instance, the ridgepole incident is discounted in recent, documented versions, and the Adobe Walls saloonkeeper, Jim Hanrahan, who had been warned of the attack, is credited with firing his pistol before dawn to awaken the occupants. Hoyt makes no mention of any casualties among the defenders and implies that they won the battle. However, three of them were slain. A count showed 56 horses and 28 oxen killed, the rest of the stock run off; and the Indians wreaked such destruction on the settlement that the intrepid hunters and merchants alike were forced to abandon it. Minimic, Indian medicine man, who had learned the habits of the hunters, how they slept with open doors and beside their wagons on the ground, had promised an easy victory. He fell from his horse, almost a mile from the scene, the target of perhaps the longest shot on record, from buffalo hunter Billy Dixon's Sharp's 50, and was dragged away by other warriors. Chief Quannah Parker led the Comanches; Lone Wolf, the Kiowas; Stone Calf and White Shield, the Cheyennes.]

Right after this fight [on July 2], a man named Watkins was set upon and scalped by a small band of Cheyennes between King Fisher stage station and the Cimarron on the Chisholm

Trail. The same day, the Indians attacked the stage station at Red Fork, north of the river, killed three station horses, wounded one and stole two. On the 4th of July, about 50 Cheyennes, Comanches and Kiowas attacked a train of three wagons on the east bank of Turkey Creek, south of Buffalo Springs, and massacred Pat Hennessey and his three drivers. The train was hauling supplies from Wichita to Fort Sill. The drivers were killed and scalped and their bodies mutilated. The Indians took poor Pat, tore his scalp from his l ead, tied him to the hind wheel of one of his wagons, took sever·ıl sacks of oats from his wagon and spilled them around him, set fire to them, and burned him alive by this slow process. Pat had come from Ireland to Canada with his mother, two brothers and two sisters, and settled in Erinsville, Ontario, where the five children grew up. The two girls stayed in Canada, but the three boys migrated to the United States. Pat's brothers settled in Fulton, New York, but young Pat was attracted to the far West, where his career ended on the Chisholm Trail. The next day, Agent John Miles and his party, fleeing from the Cheyenne Agency at Darlington, came upon his charred remains and buried him near the scene of his tragic death.

Teamsters and stages stopped at Buffalo Springs reported seeing about 100 Indians pass to the north and east that morning. It was believed these war parties were moving toward Kansas, and everybody was ready for a fight. [After the attack on Adobe Walls, the combined Indian forces had separated; some remained in Texas, others went into New Mexico and Colorado, and still others raided along the Fort Sill–Wichita road and as far north as the Republican River in northern Kansas and southern Nebraska. The buffalo hunters were forced to suspend operations throughout the Southern Plains region, and numerous outrages and atrocities were committed among the frontier settlements. At least 190 persons were killed. An aggressive campaign against the hostiles was planned with Colonel Nelson A. Miles of the Fifth Infantry— later lieutenant general commanding the United States Army—in immediate command of the troops in the field. Besides the Fifth Infantry under Colonel Miles, the troops participating were composed of battalions or companies of the Fourth, Sixth, Eighth, Tenth, and Eleventh Cavalry under Colonel Ranald S. MacKenzie, Lieutenant Colonel Thomas H. Neil, Major William R. Price, Lieutenent Colonel John W. Davidson, and Colonel George P. Buell, respectively. The bases from which they operated were Fort Dodge, Kansas; Camp Supply and Fort Sill, Indian Territory; Fort Griffin, Texas; and Fort Bascom, New Mexico.] I thought by now Kansas could survive anything. It had been bleeding Kansas, droughty Kansas, the state of severe winters and cyclones and tornadoes, the state of cranks, and the state of mortgages. It had even survived the national panic of 1873 [brought on by the failure of the general banking business of Jay Cooke, the American capitalist, known as the "Financier of the Rebellion"]. It seemed like a land of chance. One thing the people had left was "grit," and we braced ourselves for this new outbreak of the redskins. But we were unable to cope with the new fame it suddenly achieved the summer of 1874. What little we had growing was all demolished by grasshoppers!

They came the last of July, sweeping the state from the northwest to the southeast, in large clouds that darkened the sun, and when they lit, everything green vanished. They spread into Cowley County before the close of August, completely covering the trees and fields. Whole wheat fields vanished and corn was stripped down to the stalk. They ate on peach trees until all that was left hanging were the twigs with the stones. Garden vegetables were a luxury to them, and they had such voracious appetites that melons were soon eaten down to a shell. They even chewed holes in the clothes my wife had on the line. When they lit on my box house, they never stopped for a blessing. I had to give them a load of shot every little while to save those cottonwood boards, and when they left, the house looked like I had painted it white. They cleaned up everything. There was absolutely nothing left for the settlers to live on except bread and gravy, and I named Kansas the great gravy state of the Union.

Starvation or emigration seemed the only alternatives. Everybody wanted to sell and nobody wanted to buy. Few could leave because they had not the means to get away with. The people became panic-stricken. Because of the panic of 1873, we could expect little help from the East. Governor Osborn called an emergency session of the legislature, which authorized an issue of over $70,000 in state bonds to provide relief to the grasshopper sufferers until another crop could be raised, and the Kansas Central Relief Committee [organized at Topeka in November with Lieutenant Governor E. S. Stover as chairman] solicited aid and took charge of donations. In this way large amounts of rations and clothing were distributed. It was all that kept down a general exodus. Trouble was the relief went to the most ravaged counties.

Cowley County was not included in the governor's list to the legislature, and one day as three of us destitute border men sat on a dry-goods box whittling and wondering what would become of us, I suggested a relief movement to do justice to all concerned. "If you will join me," I told my two trusties, "we will compel the state to give all us hungry fellows a job for the winter fighting Indians, and thus put a stop to all these scares forevermore, opening a new inducement for immigration to this country."

"And just how," asked one, "do you propose to bring all this about? You know Colonel Miles has already run most of them redskins clean into Texas. [On August 30, Miles had found and attacked a large band of hostiles at the headwaters of the Washita; he defeated them and drove them to the Staked Plains. Toward the end of September, Colonel MacKenzie had attacked a large village near the headwaters of Red River in Texas, capturing and destroying nearly 100 Cheyenne lodges and taking over 1,400 mules and horses. On October 9, Colonel Buell captured and destroyed a Kiowa village north of the Washita. This relentless campaign had dampened the warlike ardor of the tribes.] Troops have been stationed to guard the government trains and mail service all along the line from Caldwell to Fort Sill, and there ain't been a Indian raid this side of the Chisholm since."

"Well," said I, "all them redskins need is a little touching off. You know that camp at the head of Deer Creek? Tomorrow night

111

there will be a full moon. We all have good horses. We have good firearms and know how to use them. We'll make a dash into this camp and shoot it up a little and that will start the ball rolling. Then we'll dash into town and report a great uprising. Everybody will be alarmed and want to organize a militia to protect the border, and the state will give us money, grub, and something to do for the winter. What do you think, boys?"

They jumped up and grabbed me by the hands, declaring it a go and swearing themselves to the utmost secrecy.

The next night we sneaked out of town and soon made it to the Indian camp, and without further ceremony we charged with hideous yells, shooting in wild confusion, and such a howling of dogs and making for the brush you can only imagine. We did our work quickly and fled back to the state line, established a fort and named it Dixie, and sent messengers to notify the settlers.

Then into town we flew, spreading the alarm, and the wildest confusion prevailed. We were looking wild and our horses were played out. My horse had been shot through the upper part of the neck, and I showed the wound and blood, and no questions were asked. We at once threw a guard around Fort Dixie, and the settlers poured in all night for safety. I remember one old fellow came, pounding his oxen on the back, and as he drove into Thompson's barn with their tongues hanging out, where we had a light, and jumped out of his cart all excited, Thompson said, "Why, man, look at yourself! Go to the well and wash off." In the four mile race to town the heat and severe exercise had caused the cattle's bowels to move, and the old man had received the results full in the face and chest.

Without going into further detail, I will simply state that a local company, affiliated with the state militia, was authorized and organized immediately. Consult the muster and pay roll of the Kansas State Militia for December, 1874, and you will find "Company A, Cowley County, Kansas Militia, Station, Arkansas City," and the membership of the unit as follows: G. H. Norton, A. J. Pyburne, A. D. Keith, W. M. Berkey, A. Chamberlain, A. M. Melton, K. E. Smith, Al Mowry, J. S. Nichols, J. C. Evans, C. L.

Couchman, C. L. "Cal" Swarts, George H. McIntire, William Wright, W. S. Thompson, W. M. Fowler, Henry "Hank" Mowry, William A. Wilson, B. G. Jones, E. J. "Buckskin Joe" Hoyt; John, Charles, and William Alexander; A. W. Bergey, William Beach, J. L. Boyd, John Breene, William Bates, E. M. "Ed" Bird, A. A. Berry, L. K. Berry, L. W. Courtier, James Coffey, R. L. Cowles, Joseph Disser, A. Davis, John Eskin, Jerry Evans, J. M. Folton, W. E. Houch, James Godfrey, B. F. Groomer, W. G. Gooch, Sam Hess, Fremont Horn, Jerome Hilton, A. C. Hilton, A. C. Holland, Stephen Jones, Frank Jones, O. P. Johnson, D. T. "Trout" Kitchen, John Laughon, D. D. Lewis, T. F. Lent, Ezra Milks, H. H. Merriam, George Nelson, Peter Pearson, A. W. Patterson, John Phillips, C. G. Richards, W. M. Seavey, H. P. Stanley, Joseph Shidler, P. T. "Pat" Somers, G. H. Shearer, Cass Turpin, Robert Wood, Frank Wood, A. B. Wolsey, W. A. Wilson, Edward Willard, Robert Washam, Charles Wilson, H. O. Ward, and L. Youst.

Norton was made Captain; Pyburne, 1st Lieutenant; Keith, 2nd Lieutenant; Berkey, 1st Sergeant; and Chamberlain, Melton, Smith, and Mowry, Sergeants. The rest were privates. I was chief scout and bugler.

After being mustered into service, armed, and equipped, we took the road to prosperity and the field for duty. We covered the border to the west, and by orders from the head of the department were not to go beyond the Chisholm Trail, so we set up headquarters and a supply camp on Bluff Creek, near the state line.

The very best material of the plains composed our company, but I must admit we were a hard-looking outfit. Many of the boys wore overalls and in most cases their seats were so thin you could see white patches of underwear. We were without overcoats so we wrapped ourselves in bright red blankets and looked very much like Indians in the saddle. I wore my buckskins and long hair and came very close to being shot as an Indian more than once. Only a similar outfit out of Medicine Lodge looked worse than we did. I named our company the "Ragged-Ass Militia," and it was so entered on state records.

The government troops continued to harass the redskins to the south and west, and thus our campaign extended into the winter. We kept busy patrolling the section and warning settlers if they saw any sign of an attack to hitch up their teams, throw their families and bedding into a wagon, and drive north to safety, that we would never be too far away to cover their retreat. As far as I know, no war parties crossed the line.

One morning we learned a large party was out after scalps south of us, and we planned to take them. Captain Norton split the company in two sections, each to take a different route and meet at the head of Skeleton Creek in the Outlet. When our half of the command reached the point agreed upon, we discovered a smoke just over the hill. One of our flankers John Laughon, reported that it looked like Keith's party, so Captain Norton advised him to go over and tell them they might as well join us. Laughon returned in a few minutes with, "By God, Cap, that's them doggone Injuns, for I seed their ponies and smelled skunk [camp]." I lit out to check for myself, and by this time they smelled us too, for when I made a sneak down a deep draw that led direct to their camp, they had packed and gone. I sighted them through my field glasses going west on the double quick, and dashed back to the Captain and reported.

He ordered us to take extra ammunition and grub, leave our supply wagon on the Skeleton for Keith's party, and cut loose. We sighted the war party from the top of a hill, still making good time with the dust flying. We kept after them until dark, waited one hour for the moon to rise, then followed their trail for a while by moonlight. I had been over the section while hunting buffalo with Johnson. I knew there was no fresh water until we reached Turkey Creek, and decided this was where they were headed. So we made camp on the prairie. I stayed out late watching for Indian fire signals. As I was returning to camp, I undertook to jump what appeared to be a little gully, and fell, horse and all, into a big slough hole. He pulled me out all right. When I reached camp, I staked him out and hunted Cap's bed, and rolled in, mud to my chin and with boots and spurs on.

Buckskin Joe as Scout and Indian Fighter in Kansas and the Indian Territory in the 1870's.

Buckskin Joe at Leadville, Colorado, in 1879.

Buckskin Joe (seated on box with his violin) with a group of miners and prospectors at their cabin in Leadville, Colorado, about 1880.

E. J. HOYT,

EXPLORER AND ALL AROUND MAN, BETTER KNOWN AS B. S. JOE,

The Frontiersman and Border Musician,

TEACHER

OF

KNOTTY NOTATION,
VIOLIN SAWING,
CLARINET SQUALLING

AND

TRIPLE-TONGUE
BACK ACTION
CORNET BLOWING.

If you don't reach it in 24 Lessons,

I guarantee most horrifying results in 24 Lessons.

vote the other ticket, and don't give it away.

B. S. JOE'S BORDER BRASS BAND

Buckskin Joe's show card as "Professor" of music in Kansas in the 1880's.

Buckskin Joe as he appeared in 1892 with his own Buckskin Joe Wild West Show.

Buckskin Joe as he appeared during his expedition to Nova Scotia prospecting for gold in 1884. As he left the train, a little girl spied his long hair and ran to her mother, crying, "Ma, ma, Christ has come! I saw him get off the train."

A novelty feature in Buckskin Joe's Wild West Show of 1892 was this Family Cowhorn Band. Ox horns were cut or lengthened to form a chord (bass, alto, etc.) playing the "on and after time" to Joe's aria on the cornet. When the band was in full swing, it sounded like a steam calliope. (With Joe in the photo are his three daughters and a son-in-law. Second from right is Joe's wife, Belle. Children in front are Dr. Vance Hoyt of Topanga, California, and a cousin.)

William Palmer, "Butcher-knife Bill," was Joe's partner at Leadville, Colorado. (They exchanged shots in the Civil War during the Peninsular Campaign of 1862, met again at Leadville during the silver strike, and became friends for life.)

Ella Hoyt (Joe's daughter) as she appeared in Joe's Wild West Show of 1892. (Ella was the mother of Dr. Vance Hoy of Topanga, California. She married Eddie Blubaugh, who was killed in the Oklahoma land rush of 1889, the year Dr. Hoyt was born. Afterwards, Vance was adopted and reared by his grandfather, Buckskin Joe. Ella later became a dramatic actress.)

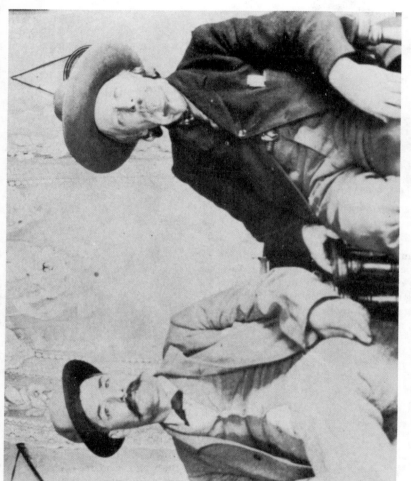

William "Butcher-knife Bill" Palmer and Buckskin Joe just before their departure into the jungles of Honduras in 1897.

When Cap awoke next morning, I was a fright to behold. "Doggone your picture!" he said. "When did you get in here, and how did you get all that 'air mud over you?" And one of the boys spied my horse and shouted out, "Oh, just see Joe's horse, they sure must've been after him last night!"

I cleaned my buckskins the best I could, and after breakfast we took the trail to Turkey Creek. We scouted down its course through the timber and found nothing but plenty of turkey, wolves, and some Cheyenne corpses rolled tight in buffalo hides and slung up in the trees, which was their method of burial. We shot a couple of turkeys and did some target practice along the creek, but not the first redskin showed his feathers. They had taken the wise course southwest to the Cimarron and crossed into the reservation. After a short rest and a good meal, we went back to the Skeleton, picked up Keith's party, and started for the border.

About 35 miles from the line, we stopped for the night, and as was my habit, I was sleeping a little apart from the others when I opened my eyes to see a big prairie wolf standing over me looking square down in my face with a grin I did not admire. I knew better than to make a quick move. Slowly and with great caution I pulled my six-shooter from under my blanket, and in a flash, shoved it into his face and fired, at the same instant springing to my feet. The wolf, badly wounded and dazed, stampeded the whole camp. By the time everybody stopped yelling and shooting, he was so full of holes he wouldn't hold mud.

In the confusion, Laughon, thinking it was an attack, mounted his horse and struck for the hills, lost his bearing, and had to lay out the rest of the night. At daybreak, I took a small squad and set out to find him. It was a cold morning with a biting north wind, and we had our red blankets around us. About 9 o'clock we sighted his white horse following a government bull train that was headed north for Wichita. The instant they spotted us, they corralled for a fight.

We stayed out of range, and I told my men, "Laughon has probably told them of our great Indian battle, and they have been expecting an attack. Somehow we have to make them know who we are."

So I threw off my blanket, and holding a white handkerchief up on the barrel of my carbine, advanced alone in my buckskins. Laughon recognized me at once; the bullwhackers raised up from behind their wagons, and the boss called out, "Dang your hide, Joe, I came nigh parting your hair."

Laughon came to meet me, shivering with the cold, and seemed mighty glad to get back to camp for a cup of hot coffee and thaw out.

Spring came and the Indian war was over. The government troops had kept the redskins on the move all winter, and they had no time to hunt buffalo for meat and robes. Hungry and half-clad, most of them surrendered at Fort Sill and Darlington. The rest were captured and their lodges destroyed. The leaders were finally sent to prison at Fort Marion, Florida, and the others agreed to bury the hatchet. We agreed to do the same.

We went back to Arkansas City and disbanded the Ragged-Ass Militia. If the people had known how that fight was brought on at the time we organized, I and my friends would have stretched rope. Now they see it in a different light, for the money it brought in kept many from starving. I hope my readers will not criticize me too harshly.

CHAPTER XI

*My Return to Show Life, Traveling with
the Laiscell Family Troupe as Bert Laiscell,
"King of the High Rope"—Mining and
Prospecting in Colorado, Trouble-Shooting
for "Haw" Tabor—Caught in the Ute
Indian Uprising of 1879, and a Race for
Life*

We were through with the Indians, but we still had the grasshoppers. They had reached down from the Platte in Nebraska
into northern Texas and east into Missouri and laid eggs in
favorable locations over the whole territory. The young hatched
in the spring, and by May, they were thick in the wheat and other
crops. Relief funds had been exhausted. Thousands of people
would have sold everything they owned for a sixth of what it
would have been worth if it hadn't shrunk in value and left the
state, if they could have found purchasers. Many left anyway.

Those who stayed devised all sorts of contraptions to kill off
the insects. Special boxes were built on reaper platforms, and the
farmers drove over the fields, filling their boxes every few minutes.
They dumped the hoppers in huge piles and burned them. The
state legislature authorized trustees of the different townships and
the mayors of the cities not included in any township to direct
overseers of the road districts to call out all able-bodied males
between the ages of 12 and 65 to destroy the pests. Persons over
eighteen could pay $1 per day and be exempt, but those who failed
to answer the call or pay the stipulated amount were fined $3 per
day.

The settlers turned out in huge companies to fight the hoppers
with brush brooms, clubs, blankets, and pitchforks. Many carried

117

shotguns and advanced against the enemy as if into battle, led by brass bands that gave out a tinny, off-key rendition of a military march. Whether it was the shotgun blasts or the off-key music that caused the hordes to flee in front of these armies I do not know, but the pests did flee in great clouds. In June, having passed into the winged state, they suddenly rose into the air and disappeared. We never knew where they went, but that was the end of the grasshopper plague.

It began to rain, and Kansas waked to a new life and hope. Immigration set in again. Houses that had been emptied were retenanted. The second and third plantings that spring furnished those products that astonished millions at the Kansas exhibition held at the World's Fair in Philadelphia. Thousands visited the state on tours of observation, and some stayed. But all spent money, and made times better.

We went back onto our respective ranches with renewed energy and faith. Many sold out to new arrivals. I trapped, hunted, and played for dances that winter, trying to raise money to start a Wild West show with the Big Hill Osages and Indian trader Ed Finney as their interpreter, but failed, so I sold my ranch and moved to town. In the spring of 1877, I bought the Berry Brothers' Indian Trading Post and changed its name to the Athletic Grocery, with Frank Spears as my partner. We built a gymnasium in the back, where we put in more time than we did in the store. If a customer wanted anything, he could help himself and leave the money on the counter. But we did a good business, and I had some fun.

I remember once we had an opposition on sugar, and I secured a barrel of fine white sawdust and mixed molasses with it, producing a fine imitation of brown sugar which I advertized twenty pounds for a dollar, with a sample in the window. A lady from the country came in, saw the sample and my sign, and asked to see some of it. I showed her the sample. Before I could stop her, she had a big wad of it in her mouth and came near choking to death. I gave her the big laugh, and she gave me the devil. She never came back, and I didn't blame her.

One day a big Osage came in, and I picked up a red pepper bottle and pretended to drink from it. The Indian commenced to beg for a drink of *pedseni* [the Osage name for liquor], so I handed him the bottle, and said, "Drink quick—heap firewater." He grabbed it, and the second swallow took his breath. He dropped the bottle with a big grunt. Out the door he went and down the street, and as far as I could see he was going with his G-string sticking out straight behind. He never came back for any more *pedseni*.

One hot forenoon in the summer of 1878, when all was quiet, four well-armed men rode into town, fed and watered their horses, then came to my store and ordered a big lunch of crackers, cheese, and bologna. I soon recognized one of them as Jesse James.

I hadn't seen Jesse before, but his description had been in the papers for years. Since the war, he had robbed banks and trains in Missouri and Kentucky and from Texas to Minnesota. After the Northfield disaster, he was supposed to have gone to Mexico. As a boy he had suffered granulated eyelids, and the rest of his life had the involuntary habit of blinking. He had large eyes, of a light shade of blue. And they were blinking fast at me at the moment.

We joked a little, and he said he had seen me in a circus once in Iowa. About noon he paid for the lunch all round. As he started out, he shook my hand with the remark, "I will see you again sometime, Joe."

A few minutes later I saw all four men ride past my store up the street. Three of them stopped on the west side at the bank, and the fourth rode up a block further, dismounting and pretending to fix his saddle. The three hitched their horses and entered the bank, leaving one man at the door. Jesse stepped up to the cashier, the only person on duty at that time of day, and threw down a twenty for change. As the cashier reached for the twenty, Jesse threw back a handkerchief covering his hand, exposing a six-shooter pointed at his head. The second man also stepped up and covered him.

Jesse led the cashier into a back room where he ordered him to "sit down and take it easy." The second man rushed into the vault and helped himself to about $3,000. Meanwhile, the man at the door did some fine work keeping a customer from entering by asking him questions about those horses tied in front. After taking the money, they left their prisoner in the doorway, mounted, and joined the fourth man up the street, then all made quick time out of town, going northwest along the river to my old ranch. The next thing I saw was Fred Farrar, the cashier, running bareheaded down the street, hollering at the top of his voice, "They have robbed the bank! They have robbed the bank!"

The president, who was home eating dinner, came like a rushing wind, and all was excitement. A posse formed quickly and were soon on the trail leading into the lower side of the grove back of my old place. They surrounded the grove and sent for me. "You know every twig in them woods, Joe," they said. "We want you to go through the grove and flush them out."

I laughed at the idea of having the robbers surrounded. I told them, "Send a couple of men up north on my old hedge row and they will find their trail going west toward the river."

Sure enough, they found the trail, then wanted me to head a party to go after them. I asked, "Who will pay me? Is there a reward to justify such chances? Those fellows are armed with six-shooters and high-powered rifles. You are armed only with shotguns."

They hadn't thought of that. I led them up the river and found where the robbers had crossed at the Salt City Ferry, saving themselves the trouble of swimming the Arkansas. By that time, they were well on their way to safety. None of the James gang was ever brought back to Cowley County, but one of its members, who was tried for another crime sometime later, admitted taking part in the affair.

That summer I gave the natives a treat by walking a rope stretched across the street between the tops of the town's two tallest buildings. [Myrtle McNelly Dening, of Hobart, Oklahoma, and an early resident of Arkansas City, writing for the *Traveler* on November 23, 1910, recalled the incident: "I was only ten years old, but it seems like yesterday. Joe climbed up on Matlock's building, and after a certain amount of 'fixing' was done, he stepped out onto the rope with his long balancing pole. Our hearts came up into our throats. Yes, he was going across. Then, there he was, half way over. *Good heavens*, I thought, *he is going to fall!* But there he was, all right, and stepped onto the building across the street. Well, we rested our necks a minute and got another breath, and just as we were trying to breathe the second time, he started back, and we held that breath until he was over again, and then we laughed and cried and said, 'We wish we could walk the rope,' and many of us kids went home and tried the clothesline, without success. There was no form of entertainment other than the little church concerts and socials to divert the minds of those who were trying so hard to settle a wild country, and the free exhibitions Joe used to give were the grandest things we ever saw. And the band would play. Remember the Buckskin Band? The best that ever tooted a horn! The days Joe put on his shows were indeed gala occasions for everyone. The country people would flock into town, and all the town people were out to see. I think now how much he did for the people then."]

I became quite proficient in aerial pedestrianism. One day I pushed a wheelbarrow across the rope, stopping in the center, starting a fire in the barrow and offering to cook my dinner. On August 22, Belle gave birth to our third daughter, whom we named Flotina. I tried hard to induce her to let me carry the baby across the rope tied on my back, but failed. Flotina was born exactly at noon, hence her middle name, Noonday.

My feet itched for the show life again, so I sold my interest in the Athletic Grocery to Spears and joined the Laiscell Family troupe with a traveling show called the Occidentals. It was the greatest bill of the season, in four acts. There were serio-comic selections by Miss Nina Holly and Miss Georgie Grey. Miss Ollie Sutter amused the boys with her new song, "When There is No One By." Other favorites included Miss Jessie White in black-face songs and dances, the only lady who did that style of business; Miss Emma Cavana, the Lively School Girl; Miss Ellen Banks in

Irish Imitations; operatic selections by the petite serio-comic vocalist, Miss Blanche Trenham; Miss Clara Wagner, the Jig Champion; James Dalton in his great Old Man song, "Old Uncle Pete"; and original German songs and dances by Paus, the Dutch Lepetre. There was James Leslie, the Great Stump Orator; Professor T. A. Wiggins, the famous magician, and his Little Mysterious Table; and Elo Nino Eddie, the Boy Wonder of the Ages, in his great Pedestal Contortion Act, with a $1000 challenge to anyone who could duplicate it. There were Japanese Sports by Professor Charles Laiscell and his son, and the Grand Act Milatare, with Laiscell himself introducing his Lightning Zouave Drill—let all lovers of the manly art of self-defense beware. The laughable Laiscell family pantomime, entitled "The Cobler's Frolic," concluded the performance. I was billed separately as "Bert Laiscell, King of the High Rope," with hair cut short, a plug hat, and gold-headed cane. Starting from Emporia, Kansas, I made daily high rope walks with this company, traveling over six states, winding up in Colorado the spring of 1879.

Several things happened on this trip which I should mention. At St. Joseph, Missouri, I had a dangerous attack of erysipelas that laid me up for a week. The doctor worked hard to keep it from going to my brain. It caused us to cancel our date there, but I caught up with the troupe at Sioux City, Iowa, and I walked the rope that night. My balancing pole broke in two, but I got home with half of my pole gone.

It was here that Mrs. Laiscell, after making a few ascents over the circus tents and watching me so much, became conceited enough to insist on trying to make a walk to the top of a six-story building. So we advertized her as the Female Blondin, Bert Laiscell's sister.

Night came and everything was in readiness. Thousands of people gathered to see this daring attempt made by a woman. I had the rope trussed back center of the old Olympic Theater, eighteen feet above its flat roof. The announcement was made, and she made her appearance at the top of the building, dressed fit to kill. I helped her to the end of the rope and gave the signal, and the band began to play. She rose with her balancing pole, then froze in position.

"They are waiting for you," I said. "You had better go."

Finally she replied, "I cannot take the first step—I am paralyzed."

I could see she had been overcome by the height and the penalty. I yelled to the announcer, "Tell the people the great Female Blondin has suddenly taken sick and cannot appear, but that her brother Bert, King of the High Rope, will make the walk in his street clothes."

I pulled off my shoes and slipped on my walking pumps. At the signal, "Ready," the band struck up, and I made a running dash out onto the rope and never stopped short of center. The band came up the street and stopped under me and played, and a big cheer went up. I danced on the rope and made a good deal of fun and was a big hit with everyone, for the following appeared in the newspaper a few days after we left Sioux City: "The rope walking mania is raging to a fearful extent just now, and about one half the back yards in the city are supplied with ropes stretched from fence to fence on which young America spends its time trying to imitate Bert Laiscell. Last Sunday a number of boys gave a sort of public performance in the pound, and it is probable these amateur efforts will be kept up until a few of these young aspirants retire with dislocated limbs or broken necks."

At Minneapolis, in October, I performed the difficult feat of walking over St. Anthony Falls, two-hundred feet in mid-air, and many who witnessed it saw fit to present me with a new rope costing $50. We went to Dakota, appearing at Yankton on April 3, 1879, then into Nebraska, and at Sidney Barracks, this rope was used to stretch the neck of a Texas desperado. His name was Charley Read, alias Douglas, a member of Doc Middleton's gang of horse thieves. On May 10, Read struck down with his six-shooter and shot a young man named Henry Loomis over a woman. The young man died in the hospital at the Barracks that afternoon.

Read was arrested and incarcerated. About 11 o'clock that

night, just as we finished our show, about 400 people seized my rope and went to the jail, demanding the prisoner. They over-powered the guards and compelled the sheriff to give up the keys, then tied Read's hands behind him and led him to Front Street with the rope around his neck and one boot on. A ladder was procured and placed against a telegraph pole on the south side of the Union Pacific track. The rope was passed over the arm of the pole, and with six men on the end of it, Read was asked if he had anything to offer.

He said, "Give me 30 feet start and a good six-shooter, and that is all I ask."

The spokesman said, "That you can't have, but we will give you a choice of being drawn up by the rope, or walk up the ladder and be swung off."

"Well," said he, "as long as it makes no difference, I believe I will walk up the ladder."

Before he started, I stepped in and laid my hand on his shoulder to lend him encouragement. But there was not a shake or a shiver. He walked up seven rounds in that condition, and when he struck the seventh, stopped, got his balance, and in a strong, calm voice, said, "Good bye, gentlemen," and bounded off with great energy.

He came down and never kicked once. His neck was broken.

They cut him down at 3 o'clock in the morning and carried him into the back room of a saloon and held an inquest. The verdict was suicide—death by his own hand—as he had jumped from the ladder with his own effort. I cut the knot from the end of the rope, and still have it.

At Denver, a few weeks later, that same rope almost plunged me into eternity. We played there two weeks and I walked it every night, trussed eighteen feet above the theater. I performed for the first time the daring feat of balancing on my head. I also played a cornet solo and marched to the time across the rope, stopping in the center, and was dancing to the music when the strands all broke or pulled in two except one, almost sending me to my death.

It was here, also, that our treasurer was charged with bigamy.

With three cases against him, he captured our bank roll and skipped. But I managed to contract with Miss Mabel Rivers for the Laiscell family to go to Leadville and open in her New Athenaeum Theater on State Street, and thus saved the show.

On our arrival at Fairplay, the terminus of the railroad, I told the boys that we would have to end our plug hat business, that we must now change to a rough life and mingle with rough characters, and plug hats were good only for the Leadville miners to shoot at.

From Fairplay, we took the stage 21 miles by Mosquito Pass and arrived in the teeming little city, dusty and tired, but on schedule. Miss Rivers gave us a big reception; we took over full management of the theater, and started off with large houses. The Laiscell family made a big hit and soon became great favorites, and myself, Bert Laiscell, King of the High Rope, was a wonder. I made 28 walks in this place, and had a new feature every night. I walked the rope with a hoop around my feet, blindfolded, and with my head tied in a sack, and announced to walk it with my adopted sister, Mrs. Laiscell, each of us starting on opposite sides of the street at the same time and passing in the middle.

The buildings here were quite low. I felt sure she could make this walk, and she agreed to try once more. So I advertized a great double walk, and the people began to argue that it was a fake, that it could not be done. "Two trains can't pass on the same track," they said, and the papers commented on it. The whole camp turned out to witness what most believed an impossibility.

The band struck up, and we made our appearance on each side of the street in gay costumes. At the roll of the drum, we started. The excitement grew as we approached each other. Then, to the amazement of all, I dropped, swinging myself under the rope by one hand and allowing her to pass over me. Then I cautiously drew myself back to my feet, completing my journey, and the shout went up: "Easy enough, *if you have the nerve!*"

We soon engaged a couple of aerial performers, Leo and Humes, who were billed with the Laiscell family, but Humes was taken sick, and I went on with Leo to set this act going. Everything went fine all week, but on Saturday night, in doing my finish—a swinging somersault across the dome blindfolded—Leo caught me by the wrists as usual, but in throwing me for the reverse, missed my feet, leaving me in space head down.

I fell like a shot, landing on my head and right shoulder on top of the piano, cutting a five-inch gash in my scalp and smashing a violin to pieces. But I was back on my feet at once, grabbing the running rope and climbing hand over hand to the dome and back on my perch with the blood spurting. By this time there were a dozen men in the boxes with six-shooters leveled on Leo and demanding to know whose fault it was.

Charley Laiscell rushed onto the stage, shouting, "Please gentlemen—do not be hasty!" And I sang out from my perch to Leo, "I am coming again," and to the men with the six-shooters, "If he lets me fall this time, *shoot to kill.*"

Leo dropped to his single bar, regaining his composure, and I shot across the dome through the air to him. And you can bet he caught me that time!

I slid back to the stage on the running rope and collapsed from loss of blood. They carried me into the wine room where a doctor from the audience stopped my bleeding and sewed up my head, then a cab took me to the hotel. Within four days, I was back on the stage again.

This was the summer of 1879, and the James boys had arrived in town. I did not suppose they would know me in my disguise, but the very first evening, Jesse stepped up to me, and slapping me on the shoulder, said, "Hello, old friend."

"Your pardon, sir," said I. "I am not an acquaintance of yours."

He stared at me impatiently for a few moments, and remarked, "Well, I'll be doggoned if I didn't take you for my old friend, Buckskin Joe, and I was wondering what you was doing dressed up in all that frumpery. I'll be gosh hanged if I wasn't."

Then, in a voice loud enough for the crowd to hear, he said to one of his boys, "Bob, were you ever mistaken for anybody?"

"Yes," replied "Bob", with a grin. "I was stepping off the train one day, and a passenger came up to me, saying, 'Jesus Christ, I'm glad you let me keep my wallet.'"

The boys laughed, and Jesse asked me to have a glass of beer with him. He asked again what I was doing with my hair "all cut off" and "them dude clothes on," and I told him I was now Bert Laiscell, King of the High Rope, and had charge of the New Anthenaeum Theater.

"Joe," he said, "we appreciated you giving us cheese and crackers for the trail last year, and I will appreciate you giving us a private box in your theater tonight."

I agreed to arrange it. "When you come in, send for Bert Laiscell, and I will be on tap."

When they arrived, I gave them a fine box and a private waiter. They dropped about $200 that night for tips, 25-cent cigars, and wine at $7 per bottle. Good customers! When they left town, I sure hated to see them go.

While devoting my nights to the theater, I devoted my days to prospecting. Nearly every merchant, lumberman, mechanic, and professional man in Leadville, though they had all the business they could attend to, was engaged in mining and prospecting as a sideline. They would grubstake someone to sink a shaft for them while they continued to follow their own calling, and there were numerous instances of backers retiring in a few months with a fortune. I grubstaked a good many boys, but it never amounted to anything. So I started sinking on prospects myself for an interest.

Right off I had a piece of bad luck. I was sinking a shaft at the head of Birdseye Gulch. I had one man in camp and two working the shaft half a mile away. They were down about 25 feet, one man in the shaft, one at the windlass on top. The top man was throwing on dynamite for a shot, and it exploded, blowing his bowels out, and the poor fellow crawled to the shaft to pull out his partner, but his partner yelled for him to go back, that it would fall in and kill him. The poor fellow crawled away from the shaft and died. The man at camp gave the signal for dinner, and no one came, so I went up to see why the delay and discovered the horrible sight. I pulled the man out of the shaft and abandoned the project.

In all, I sank about 22 holes from 25 to 125 feet deep, and only struck it in one shaft. This was on the Black Bird Lode, in the California District of Lake County, the sample ore assaying: silver, five ounces, coin value $5.55, and gold, two-tenths ounce, coin value $4.13. I was offered a good sum for my interest and refused. Then I got into a scrape with some claim jumpers. I brought suit, lost it, and finally came out with nothing. I decided courts were the wrong place to deal with claim thieves. A short time later, I fought a bunch of them all one night to save the Odonivan Racer Lode, and gained for myself a wide reputation.

When Horace A. W. "Haw" Tabor, the "Silver King," had a mine jumped on Carbonate Hill, he came to me with a proposition of $500 to recapture it for him. I took the contract and selected two good men. Late in the evening we spread in a half circle around the hill. When all was ready, we opened fire on the guards, and the battle was on. Before we had shot a box of ammunition, they fled, leaving us in full possession. I turned the mine over to Tabor the next morning under heavy guard.

On July 30, 1879, I contracted with Major Thomas C. Houghton to sink a shaft or run a tunnel on the Dice Box Lode a depth or length of 100 feet, unless in the meantime what was commonly termed "pay mineral" should be reached. Houghton was an old showman, a great favorite in Leadville, professionally known as T. C. Howard. I also was to sink, extend, and timber the same in a workmanlike and skillful manner, according to the rule and custom of mining in that district. In consideration, I was to receive a one-half interest. I went to work, and in a few days reached pay mineral, and had named the mine "Louise" and sold my interest to the Major when he learned that his claim had been jumped.

For what happened next, I quote from the Leadville *Chronicle*: "Major Howard immediately took a horse, and accompanied by Buckskin Joe, went to look after matters. On reaching the shaft he was halted, but kept on without any attention to the order, when an advance guard raised a gun and demanded, 'Who the hell are you?' Howard drew his revolver with the remark, 'I'll show you who I am if you don't get out of that hole damned quick.' The guard covered him with a rifle, but Buckskin Joe immediately and with lightning rapidity raised his carbine and fired, striking the stock of his opponent's gun, when the guard turned and fled, followed by two others. When at a short distance, one of them turned and fired a revolver at the Major, striking him in the side, glancing off through his overcoat, inflicting a flesh wound. Howard then placed a guard over the claim, came to town where Dr. Cook attended his wounds, which are inconsequential, and the two repaired to the Clarendon [hotel] for supper, meeting many friends who had no suspicion that such an ordeal had been passed. A clue has been found to the assailants who will probably be arrested in a few days." But we never saw them again in the district.

I don't think there was ever a tougher or more ambitious camp than Leadville at that time. It was the metropolis of the carbonate region—as one enthusiastic correspondent chose to call it, "the marvelous city set in a sea of silver." It had jumped up and grown like magic on the almost level plain between two of the grandest ranges of mountains on the continent, four miles from the valley of the Arkansas, and was building up the gulches and hills on every side. Building sites worth $25 when the carbonate of lead locations were discovered quadrupled in value, and lands along Chestnut Street and Harrison Avenue, the business thorough-fares, sold from $100 to $250 per foot of front. There were stores, large and small, restaurants, saloons, dancehalls and gambling houses at every hand, three hotels, three banks, fourteen or fifteen saw-mills, and two large smelters. There was about 20,000 people, and more still coming. We always had from three to six men for breakfast, and whenever we heard the crack of a gun, we could be sure it was something more important than someone shooting a cat or dog just for fun.

The nearly 150 licensed saloons, gambling houses, and dance halls ran full blast day and night. Few of the lucky miners saved the money they made. They squandered it in carousals or played it away as fast as they took it. The smallest piece of change was 25 cents, and that would buy only a glass of beer or a box of matches. Leadville by lamplight sparkled and boomed like one great 4th of July celebration. And there were probably more thugs, pick-pockets, and fancy women congregated there than in any one place on earth. Men were robbed within the shadows of their own doors, in their own bed-chambers, and if one's duties compelled him to be abroad late at night, he walked with a naked pistol in his hand and took to the middle of the street to keep from being ambushed at some dark corner. It would have been startling to know the actual number who were set upon in the dark dens and alleys, killed, put in a box, and buried in unmarked graves in the city cemetery. Arguments usually ended in knifings, shoot-outs, and free-for-alls. Men fought on the streets, in saloons, in dance halls, in hotels, and at the theaters. Fights drew little attention, but they kept life from being monotonous.

All in all, Leadville was a great show town, and the best performers came from all over the country. The Carbonate Concert Hall, a variety theater that boasted a Gothic window and had living pine trees that formed cozy arbors, had as its popular attractions the Lady Vienna Orchestra and Mollie Newton, "the most perfectly formed woman in America," who presented "a series of beautiful tableaux representing Greek and Roman statuary." The Grand Central Theater dazzled its patrons on its opening night with two tiers of 28 boxes handsomely curtained in lace and damask resembling cozy little parlors. Eddie Foy played there. At the Texas House, equally resplendent, the guests on its opening night, mostly agents of eastern and English capitalists, represented over $175,000,000. Amphitheaters, like the Coliseum, had bills so varied one could see anything from a wrestling match between Eugenie and Marcia to two dogs fight until one chewed the other to death. The Athenaeum advertized with a light in every window, banners floating from every point of vantage, and two great bonfires blazing from the roof.

Pop Wyman's Great Saloon drew the biggest crowds. His three-story frame building was designed as a combination saloon, gambling house, dance hall, and variety theater. There were even rooms for private parties. A quiet, ministerial-looking fellow, he never allowed a married man to gamble, and never served a drunk man at the bar. He had a large Bible chained to a mahogany pulpit inside the swinging doors, and a big sign, "Please Don't Swear." In the dance hall above the orchestra, he had another sign, "Don't Shoot the Piano Player—He's Doing His Damnedest."

He was the "dad" of the camp and a great friend of mine, and it was through his son that I signed a contract with the Atchison, Topeka and Santa Fe railroad to walk the rope, 2000 feet high, over the Grand Gorge of the Arkansas. The distance was no further than across Niagara River, which was so often traversed by Blondin, and an estimated 100,000 people from all parts of the country witnessed my unparalleled performance.

As my identity was now known, I quit the role of Bert Laiscell, let my hair grow long, and went back to my buckskin clothes. I then joined a man named Jack White to explore the Ute Indian country in western Colorado.

We loaded our burros with a few of the necessities of camp life, picks, powder, hammers, and drills, and started into this thinly inhabited region, determined to create wealth both for ourselves and others. We packed via Twin Lakes over the Sawatch Range through the pass to Independence and into the Frying Pan, through Aspen, scanning every rock formation, the granites and quartzites, the carboniferous and silvrain line ledges, the eruptive porphyry dykes. Not a seam or crevice escaped our eager eyes. We discovered several specimens of free gold of a high grade and staked several claims. Buckskin Gulch, in the Elk Mountain District, still bears my name.

Following down Eagle River, I discovered the great Springs, now called Glenwood, and planned to locate on them, but was beat out of them by a Leadville man named Blake, who sold out later for $30,000, and thereby missed another opportunity for a fortune.

We scouted the country over, and in October, a wild cry rang through the country that the Indians on the White River Reservation had gone on the warpath, murdered their agent, Nathan Meeker, and all his employes, and escaped into the wilds of the mountains, carrying with them three white women and two children. On the heels of this came the news that Major Thomas Thornburgh and a force of more than 150 soldiers, sent to White River from Rawlins, Wyoming, had been attacked from the sage ridges above Milk Creek valley. Thornburgh and eleven troopers lay dead, nearly 300 army horses and mules had been put out of action, and Chief Douglas, with all his White River Utes, had fled as conquerors. Chief Ouray, of the Los Pinos Utes, was at his winter quarters on the Uncompahgre. Chief Douglas notified him at once of his great victory and urged him to arise and lead his warriors on a great and lasting triumph.

[Ouray was a mountaineer, fighter, politician, cosmopolite, but he was an Indian with all the instincts of his race. By treaty he had gained most of Colorado's Western Slope for his people, but the rapid increase in the state's population had brought a huge demand for more land. The land-grabbers had tried to destroy the good reputation of the Indians by accusing them of outrage and theft and deliberately setting hundreds of forest fires. Frederick W. Pitkin, Colorado's new governor, had been elected on a Ute-Must-Go platform, and Senator Henry M. Teller had forced them to sell thousands of acres of prime farm land and never paid them the promised money.]

Ouray's ambition was aroused. All the fighting blood of his ancestors called him to go. How his heart longed to reclaim the lands and homes of his people, but his good wife, Chipeta, whom he loved with a true and loyal devotion, knelt at his feet, and hanging on his arm, weeping and praying, asked him to halt the depredations before all was lost and thousands of whites, their women and children, lay scalped and bleeding and mutilated beyond recognition.

All night he never closed his eyes, but tramped to and fro in his tent, and sat musing before his fire. By morning his mind was made up: "The white men have cheated and betrayed. They have torn the sides of our beloved mountains in their mad search for gold. They drove us from our happy and contented homes. No; they are as the leaves upon the trees, my children. You kill some, more come. No, no; we must live in peace with our white brothers."

Chief Douglas told the young men of the tribes that Ouray was "heap too much white man's friend." But the Chief of all the Utes was obeyed, and the war was over.

Jack and I were headed for the agency on White River to pick up supplies when the attack was made. We tried to gather a few prospectors and go to the rescue, but no one had any ammunition to speak of, and as the Indians were numerous, well-mounted, and well-armed and had already fired the agency and were after us, it was every man for himself and get away. Everyone fled for Leadville, as the winter snow was due and it would block their crossing the Divide.

Jack and I, knowing the country, made a night march above timberline, and they lost our trail. About daybreak they spotted us again, and we gave them a few shots, then changed location and baffled them, which gave us clear sailing into the mountains, which I assure you we took advantage of. High in the mountains, we stopped to rest. Suddenly we heard the brush cracking and rocks rolling below us. We grabbed our rifles and each took a tree for defense. The noise kept coming. Our pack animals snorted and bunched together. Then, into our camp stumbled a prospector, frightened out of his wits, his face and hands bleeding and his clothes all but gone.

"Come on, come on," he cried. "They are are after us! Thirty have been killed, forty more wounded, and they almost scalped me. Which way to Leadville?"

I gave him directions, and away he went, still urging us to come on, that the Utes would be on us before nightfall.

We finally pulled for the head of timberline, arriving at dusk and picking up three pack animals the old fellow had abandoned with their saddles still on. I felt safe now, as we were on the Divide. We shot a deer the next morning, packed the meat on our burros, and started for Leadville. That night we camped on Lost Man's Gulch, three miles from Independence, in a heavy fog.

After supper, Jack spotted some lights going up and down the mountain before us, and swore they were Indian signals. "Them damned Utes have us surrounded!"

"I do not think so," said I. We watched the lights bobbing for some time. Suddenly one broke away, traveling along the creek opposite our camp. This startled Jack. "We're cut off," he said. "We are in for it!"

"Well," said I, "we will settle it. I'll just shoot out that light."

"For God's sake, don't do it," begged Jack. "You will expose us."

But I pulled up my rifle and drew a good bead. Just as I was about to touch the trigger, the light disappeared.

"There now, what do you think of that?" I asked.

"It's spooky, Joe."

Finally I told him, "They are nothing to worry about. I've seen them many times along the river bogs in Canada. My old grandpa called them phosphorescents."

Jack still wasn't convinced, but I got him to roll up in his blankets and sleep with one eye open and let the lights have their fun.

By morning all was dead calm, and the snow commenced to come down in chunks. We packed to Independence and found the little camp deserted, not a soul, and the mountain all ablaze. We now had a better explanation for the lights we had seen the night before. The populace had fled, foolishly firing the timber to keep the Indians from crossing the pass.

We started the climb. The smoke was so dense our animals would bunch up with their noses to the ground to breathe, and we were forced to lie with our faces to the ground until it cleared again. Then we would whip up and struggle as long as we could, and down we would all go again for breath. At one time we were completely surrounded by fire, and it looked pretty tough, but I spotted an opening as the smoke raised, and we made a desperate rush, coming out at the head of the burning timber.

The snow was now about 12 inches deep and still coming thick and fast. It was another struggle to get through the snow over and down into Twin Lakes Gulch. We found a deserted miner's cabin and turned in for the night. Next morning the snow was two feet deep on the level. We packed, put old Beecher, our lead animal, on the trail and started behind him. He followed that trail all day, two feet under the snow, crooked and dangerous as it was. At dark we reached Twin Lakes, and early the next morning packed and started on the final lap to Leadville.

Everyone was surprised at our arrival. The town was in mourning, for that crazy duck who had made our camp in the Ute country had told all and sundry that we had been caught by the Indians and massacred. Our friends looked at us as if we had just been resurrected.

CHAPTER XII

More Colorado Experiences and Hair-Breadth Escapes, 1880–1883—My Expedition to Nova Scotia in Search of a Lost Gold Mine

As the snows had set in, I went home to Kansas for the winter, and found Cowley County experiencing a "gold rush" of its own. In the quartz hills, or mounds, east of town on the Walnut, traces of gold and silver had been discovered, and three quarter sections in the area had been leased by a mining company. Considering myself a fair expert in such matters, I went up to look over the grounds, and had to admit the formation was, to every appearance, the same as at Leadville.

My opinion was given such publicity in the Arkansas Valley *Democrat* that it nearly caused an exodus of the population from the county seat at Winfield to Arkansas City. The next week, hot off the press of the Winfield *Courier*, came this fiery counter-attack: "We do not see what is the use of inventing such frauds. Is it possible that anyone is fool enough to actually buy land in the vicinity because of the gold and silver story?"

To which the next week's *Democrat* made the following dignified and temperate reply: "What is the use of a man making an ass of himself and showing his vindictive hate to a sister town by uttering a wilful, malicious lie, like old 'blubber mouth' [the editor] of The Courier? The old man is so blinded by prejudice against Arkansas City that he cannot tell the truth. Old Growler may snarl and whine as he pleases,

137

but the quartz is to be seen here in inexhaustible quantities."

I think there really was gold in them hills at that time. Assays indicated both gold and silver in profitable quantities. Trouble was, the expense of obtaining it was such that the workings finally had to be abandoned. But the experiment caused plenty of excitement while it lasted.

Anyway, Arkansas City had something better to get excited about. The Santa Fe railroad brought its first train into the town, ending a ten-year fight on the part of its citizens for transportation and symbolizing the start of what today is the city's largest single industry.

A group of far-seeing citizens had put up $50,000 worth of land for right-of-way. Later they raised $10,000 cash for building the station, and contributed a total of 50 acres of land for the railroad's shops. The first train pulled into town from the north on January 2, 1880, almost exactly ten years from the day of the founding of the townsite. That day, Arkansas City's development as a railroad division point instead of merely the end of another branch line was settled.

The railroad played a major role in attracting settlers to this country. Through passenger trains ran from Kansas City to Atchison to the Rocky Mountains—the only direct route to the most wonderful mountain regions in America. It was the land hunters' and gold hunters' road. But thousands still went by wagon train. Early in the spring of 1880, I hired out to guide a party 600 miles across the plains and up the valley of the Arkansas, the short and dangerous route to Leadville.

The first night we camped at Wellington, Kansas. The next morning, as we were ready to pull out, a man came running toward me, hollering, "Hey, hey, there!" As I was about to mount, I waited until he caught up, and he asked, "Hain't your name Hoyt?" And I at once recognized J. T. Johnson, my old circus manager.

He said, "Come down to my stable, Joe, and see my circus horses and my wife, Edith."

I went down to the stable with him and looked over the finest bunch of circus stock I had ever seen. Then he took me overhead to see his wife, and she did not know me.

"Why, Edith," he said, "don't you remember that little bow-legged cuss who used to tumble so, the first to accomplish a double and triple somersault—one of the Canadian Brothers?"

"Oh, yes, yes!" she exclaimed. "Can it be possible?"

"All things are possible," said I, and they wanted me to go on the road with them again.

But I said, "No. I am off to the mountains, and goodbye circus." I mounted and galloped back to the wagons.

There was a mischievous, but tough little character with the train named Leonard. One night in Arkansas City he had exchanged babies on a couple of young mothers who were attending a ball I was playing for, and they never noticed it until they reached home, nearly six miles in the country. As we swung down the street, Leonard stopped at a store that had a large stuffed mountain lion on the sidewalk in front, dismounted, and picked up the lion's tail, drawing his knife at the same time and looking up at me with the remark, "Where shall I cut her off, Joe?"

I said, "Close up," and off it came, so close to the body that the sawdust was running out. He threw me the tail, and I tied it around my hat, and a shout went up all along the line. The storekeeper ran out, cursing and threatening us with damages. We rode off, and how he came out I never knew.

It was wild, desolate country from there to Dodge City, with nothing except buffalo chips for fuel. But Leonard was a good rustler. He kept us in plenty of chips, and ate from twelve to sixteen biscuits every meal. I named him the Champion Biscuit Eater of the Plains.

Heading west from Dodge, we made one drive of 140 miles without water. We made this all right by packing all the water we could and letting the stock drink only at night, and by ten o'clock the third day, reached a little stream [the Purgatory, or Las Animas, River] putting into the Arkansas near Fort Lyons. We crossed the river here and followed it to Canon City, crossing again at Canon City and over the Iron Mountains, striking it again at South Arkansas [now Salida], thence up the river to Granite, and on twenty miles to Leadville, making the 600 mile drive without a hitch in 28 days.

All the old-timers were glad to see me back. Jack White almost jumped with joy. He had been laid up in the hospital most of the winter, but promised to meet me over the range as soon as the snow disappeared. The last thing I did before leaving Leadville was to caution him against drinking so much. But he suffered a relapse and died a couple of weeks later.

There was great mining excitement on the Western Slope, and the rush was on to see who would get there first. The snow was deep on the Divide, but everyone was determined to risk a crossing. I selected George Shearer, one of our party and a former member of the old Ragged-Ass Militia, as a partner, and fitted out for a prospecting trip and to supply the new camps with game. In a couple of days we reached the main range and twenty feet of snow.

We found the prospectors bunched up here with all kinds of ideas and only one trail through the pass. The nights were cold, but the sun during the day was sufficient to melt the snow ten to twenty feet down at the bottom of the trail. There was no passing each other. If anything went wrong up front, you had to stand up or sit down in the slush and mud and be good-natured about it until the procession was ready to move on.

As Shearer and I were fixed for the occasion, we fell into line. We struggled two miles under heavy packs the first day, and made it to the head of timberline. There we found a spot big enough to leave the trail and camp in the snow to give man and beast a rest. Passersby advised us to come on, that we would freeze, but we dug a hole in a drift and wrapped in heavy blankets for the night. Next morning, with the crust hard enough to hold our animals, we kept out of the deep cut trail and doubled our time until the crust thawed and we had to slide into the trail and mingle in the slush and mud again.

We now had it downhill in the timber, and moved better. By night we were out of the snow. We made a big camp fire, and you can bet everyone enjoyed it. The next day we reached Independence Camp, which had created all the excitement from a discovery made there the previous fall.

Shearer and I decided to go on west. Taking up Lost Man's Gulch, we crossed a low divide into Elk Park, which I had scouted the year before, and established headquarters on timberline with the idea of loading up with elk meat for the camp. But I soon discovered a new lead in the old gulch I had named Buckskin, and located three new claims. I erected a monument of stones on one of the highest peaks, and the surveyors later took this for a bearing and named it Joe's Peak. This was on the Little Emma Lode, in Independence Mining District, Gunnison County, and is so recorded in the books at Aspen.

We then decided to explore and prospect, so we took in the Frying Pan River, the Holy Cross Forest, the great Lava Beds on Eagle River, and the North Fork—in short, we scouted the country over, finally returning to Leadville in the fall with a load of venison, which we sold for more than enough to pay our expenses and train fare back to Kansas. Shearer went back to his old trade as a carpenter, and I spent the winter at home, teaching music—cornet and violin.

In the spring of 1881, we returned to Leadville, packing early to Buckskin Gulch and Elk Park, taking with us a young lead miner from Joplin, Missouri, to assist in sinking shafts and do the assessment work on our claims. We struck good pay mineral, also locating claims on the Smokey Hill Lode, in the Independence Mining District, and on the Belle Franklin Lode, the U.S.A. Lode, the Noonday Lode, and the Gold Medal Lode, in the Elk Park Mining District. On November 25, we sold to Pop Wyman at Leadville for $16,000, packed our grips, and once more headed for the sunflower state, where I again taught music all winter.

Shearer quit the mining business for good, but not satisfied with my prosperity, I hit the grit again for the Rockies the spring of 1882, landing in Leadville on schedule and taking as a partner this time a man named Jack McClay, an old miner from Nova

Scotia with forty years experience underground. We packed for my old camp in Buckskin Gulch and Elk Park, taking the Frying Pan route, where one of our burros slipped over a bluff and went down the mountain with all our potatoes. We lost the burro, but we needed those potatoes. We camped and put in the day picking them up. The next night we reached the gulch. I showed McClay my old holdings. He thought they were a good thing, but too far from transportation, so we decided to explore the unknown.

We packed down Woody Creek to the Roaring Fork country, through Aspen to the mouth of Hunter's Creek, up the Highland to Ashcroft, where we located a copper lead, then over the Son of-a-Bitch Trail through Hell's Hole and back to Hunter's Creek, without success. In the reflection of the morning sun I discovered that all the deep holes were full of trout, so we camped and went fishing. I caught 25 large speckled trout in ten minutes. I had never found them this high before. Loaded with fish, we pulled for Independence Camp, where we sold out for expenses, and packed to Leadville.

I was standing on the street looking pretty tough and disappointed when Pop Wyman called me into his saloon and introduced me to a man named Cox. "He is a great artist from New York City," Wyman said, "and you are the man he wants."

Cox told me he was in Leadville to paint a realistic subject, and how much would I pose for?

"Nothing," said I. "All I want is a copy of the original."

"It's a go," said he. So I posed one hour a day for nine days. When he had finished, Wyman paid him $200 for the painting. He gave me a copy later, and it still hangs in my home.

I now repeated the dose and went back to sunny Kansas for the winter, and in the spring of 1883, returned to Leadville. Before I could fit out for another prospecting trip, Pop Wyman sent for me. A couple of English Lords had just arrived in camp and wanted a guide to take them where they could fish and hunt. Wyman had recommended me, so I bargained to go.

We set out with three good saddle ponies, two jacks, and plenty to eat and drink. I suspected it would be a picnic, for they were so green, and had never seen mountain game before.

The second day out I sighted a big elk across a little clearing, lying down. It was a long shot, but they wanted him, so I pulled up and "Bang!" went the old gun. The elk rose to his feet, and I fired again just as he reached the timber. We hurried through the woods, and about fifty yards up the hill found the elk dead. As I was cutting his throat, a noise came from the clearing below. The Englishmen seized their guns and down they went, and found a second elk dying. How, they wanted to know, could I kill two with only one in sight.

"Easy," said I. "The one I shot first never got up at all. Number Two elk got up and started off. My second shot got him."

They declared they had never seen such marksmanship.

We made camp a half mile away beside a little lake—a beautiful place and full of fish. I cut a couple of hams off for camp and hung the other two on a high limb. We stayed on the lake two days, and what a time we had living on trout and elk meat.

The second afternoon, I sent the boys up the hill after the other hams. I suspected they would find something there that would interest them. Within a few minutes, I heard them shooting and yelling. I grabbed my rifle and flew to the rescue, and met them coming downhill on a dead run with an old grizzly after them. I sent a bullet crashing through his skull and stopped him in his tracks. Those two Englishmen never stopped short of camp. I had a big laugh; they didn't think it so funny, but after they had plenty of bear meat to eat, they were feeling pretty good once more. They returned to Leadville with a bearskin and a couple of elk antlers, declaring it the best trip of their lives, and telling everyone I was the best shot and the greatest guide on earth.

Consequently, I was guide on several other hunting and fishing expeditions. In November, I negotiated with Martin Sullivan, an expert representing eastern capital, to go over the Divide and look at some claims on Ram's Horn Mountain before the heavy snows set in. We traveled by stagecoach to the Divide via Twin Lakes, then over the pass on sleds to Independence, now a mail route. We got saddle horses here and lit out, but soon struck deep snow and had to climb the mountain on foot. We examined the prospects, took samples, and got back to our stagecoach all right, only to meet a near disaster.

We had all taken seats, including a lady, Mrs. Mack, who occupied the settee with me, the driver snapped his whip over four good horses, and away we went. The snow which had fallen a few weeks before had thawed under the warm rays of the sun and the streams coming from the mountain sides had been detained in their downward course by the early nights and their freezing temperatures. In many places ice had thus formed in the roads. Just beyond Everett, we reached a very short turn and steep downgrade. The driver slackened the pace of his teams, but the traces on the off horse drooped out. The wheels skidded, the driver was thrown from his seat, headlong into the road, and over we went down the hill a hundred yards on the ice and snow.

Mrs. Mack was thrown completely over me and covered with the baggage, seats and robes. She was badly bruised about the head and face and her lower lip frightfully lacerated. Sullivan's cheek struck the door, almost breaking his jaw. My cartridge belt was torn and a half dozen cartridges were broken off in the center and the caps badly bent. It had caught on the coach, which in all probability saved me from being tossed clear of the vehicle and over the mountain side to my death.

When the coach had been righted, we regained our positions and drove to the Wolf Hotel, at the upper Twin lake, where Mrs. Mack received medical attention before we proceeded to Leadville. Sullivan and the lady wanted me to join them in getting after the company for damages, but I had more enjoyable ways of making money. I went back to Kansas, and that ended my Colorado career.

Three years before, I had vowed not to have my hair cut until I was worth $50,000. My hair now measured fifteen inches in length. My mustache was six inches long. I decided to have both trimmed, which I did. But I didn't give up trying to reach the $50,000 mark. While with Jack McClay in 1882, he had told me of some gold he discovered in quartz rock when a small boy in Nova Scotia. All I had to go on was the strength of his story, and the only landmark a little village called Milton.

In the spring of 1884, I took a man named Dell Hollenback, and boarded a train for the East. At St. Johns, Canada, we laid over two days, and I ran down to old Magog to see my mother and father and what changes had been made in my twenty-two years absence. I couldn't believe my eyes and senses. The whole country seemed so small and contracted. The mountains, once so grand, looked like bumps on a log compared with the Rockies, and Magog Lake looked like a frog pond.

As I stepped off the train, a little girl saw me and legged it up the depot steps into the arms of her mother, shouting, "Ma, ma, Christ has come!"

"What do you mean, child?" asked her mother.

"He has! He has! I saw Him get off the cars. I know I did. He has come!"

Well, that was one on me, but the child was not to blame. No doubt she had heard people talk of His coming, and seeing my long hair and Christly appearance, naturally thought it was true. The little thing, I must say, was sadly mistaken.

The old-timers, hearing of my arrival, rushed to greet me. They wanted me to come down to the hall and give a little talk on the great American West, but time would not permit. After a good visit, I bid my old home goodbye once more and continued my journey from St. Johns to Boston, Massachusetts.

We had to lay over there five days, so stopped with a friend of mine named Moore, who had married my brother Warren's widow, then sailed to Halifax, Nova Scotia. Through the postmaster, we learned of a place called Milton, near Liverpool, where once upon a time Americans had come and bought lumber in the tree in large quantities and erected large saw mills to cut it and ship it to the States, but the camp no longer existed.

That satisfied Dell and me. We spent six more days waiting for a boat, then sailed to Liverpool. We were not long finding the remains of Milton, and a community that was 200 years behind the times. The people had lived there so long they were related to each other. A few miles up the river, we found some fine virgin quartz croppings with well-defined, but low-grade ore.

I figured McClay's discovery was somewhere close, so we went back to Liverpool for supplies. We wanted some coffee, but all we could find was tea. This was mighty binding. There was a big crowd in the store, but nothing doing. I took down a fiddle that was hanging on the wall for sale and commenced playing, and you should have seen the commotion I kicked up. Everytime I finished a tune, Dell passed the hat, and we finally had 25 cents in pennies. Then I asked the price of cigars. The old storekeeper said, "Cent apiece," so I dumped the 25 pennies on the counter and told everyone to help themselves. The old man declared, "That's the biggest sale of cigars I ever made!" And the crowd looked surprised at such extravagance.

We were invited to stay for a native dance, and that night the fiddler came twenty miles on horseback and the woods turned out in the order of 200 years before. They danced in sets of four and the object seemed to be who could outdo the other and stay on their feet the longest. I had seen such antics as a boy, but I thought Dell would die laughing. And the fiddler! Such cat fighting and scratching and contortions I had never seen. For a little fun, I showed them I could dance some myself, and they were almost carried away. All the girls wanted to dance a round with me, and you bet I made them sweat.

Then they wanted to hear me play, and I asked the fiddler for his old gourd. He hesitated, but I told him I only wanted to give him a rest, and he finally consented. I picked the strings and tuned it up a little, then went at it with Leather Breeches and their style of pumpkin pie music, made in the pump room, and they liked to danced themselves to death. Even the fiddler danced like a maniac.

They thought I was some pumpkins now, so I did a little balancing and tumbling, and to climax my performance, a few sleight-of-hand tricks. That upset all I had done. Everyone commenced to groan and look serious and prepare to leave. The fiddler came up and told me I had scared them, that they were all going home for they thought I was a witch. Dell said, "You've done it now. We better get out of here before you are killed."

So we headed back to camp on the river. The next morning we came upon a couple of fellows with a bunch of fish laid out on two long, wide boards, and starting to cover a third. I asked what they were doing, and they said, "Trying to figure how much we will get for 80 pounds of fish at 5 cents a pound." They were laying out five fish eighty times and trying to add them up, and were really sweating over the problem.

"Well," said I, "it would be an even $4.00."

"How do you know without figuring?" they asked.

"Why," said I, "I did figure, in my head. I set down 80 for the fish and 5 cents for the amount per pound, and 5 times 80 is 400, pointing off two for cents, makes $4.00."

They looked at each other, and one said, "John, I always told ye we never knowed more than cattle."

I then showed them a sample of free gold and asked if they had ever seen anything like it. The one called John nodded, and directed us sixteen miles up the river to the camp of a Micmac Indian. "He can show ye, he has some all time."

Dell and I broke a record getting up the river. By late evening we had located our Indian. He readily showed us several pieces of beautiful white quartz with gold in it. I took some and put it to the test and it was free gold, so I asked him where he had found it.

"Oh, me find him up in hills," he said.

I asked if he would show us where he found "him."

The Indian said, "Oh, yes, me show you tonight for ten dollars."

We started through the thick timber with the Indian ahead, carrying a lantern, and after two hours of hard travel, he stopped. "Look, look, here him is, see, see!" We stooped down and looked, but all we could see was a lot of white rock.

I told the Indian, "This isn't the kind."

"Oh," he said, "me show you in the morning for ten dollars."

"All right," I said. There was no use arguing. "We will go again in the morning."

The next morning he took us up another trail, and I never

147

saw such a winding route as that Indian made. I had Dell fall behind with a hatchet and make signs on rocks and trees in case we had to find our own way out. And the old Indian came up, and said, "Oh, me find him this time. Me one of the company. Me one of the company."

I asked what he meant by "one of the company."

"Yes, they try to bar me, but soon take me in. Now me sell. They ask what I take to get out. Me take one thousand dollars, and they rid of me." At that moment we topped a little rise, and he pointed ahead. "See!"

Over the rise on the course of the lead was a neat little prospector's cabin, and just beyond, we suddenly came upon three men, two of them with a large iron mortar with a pestle fastened to a long spring pole, crushing white quartz and picking the gold out and placing it in collar boxes.

They appeared quite nervous as I approached, but I soon convinced them who I was, for they were intelligent people from Australia and ran a bank at Malipsic. They introduced themselves as the Owens brothers, and told me how two weeks before the old Indian had come into their bank with a few pieces of quartz rock and they had paid him ten dollars to lead them to the discovery. They had bought his rights for $1000 and taken out a license covering four square miles of country!

We sank in our boots. We could do nothing except pay the Indian ten dollars—he had kept his end of the bargain—and retreat in good order.

As Dell thought it too risky to return to Liverpool, we took across country to Yarmouth, and caught a boat there for Boston, the last one out for the season. I proposed to Dell to go up into Canada and show him my old trails, but he said, "No, I want to go straight home. We have lost our gold mine, and I want to get back before I lose my wife."

We agreed to flip a coin to decide it. He won, so I walked into the depot and bought two tickets for Arkansas City, arriving home no richer than when we left, except in experience, which I now value more than all the gold in Nova Scotia.

CHAPTER XIII

I Organize a New Buckskin Band and Join Pawnee Bill's Historical Wild West Exhibition

I now took a fresh look at my career as a musician. Early in March, 1885, I decided to organize a new band and orchestra, and announced my intentions as follows:

This is to be a first class band, and I wish to notify the public at large, also the profession, that good musicians are wanted and none other need apply, for I do not wish to annoy the dead or peaceful citizens of this city with amateur Jim Crow music. My receipt for a good band is good instruments, good music and a professional leader; my receipt for a failure is cheap instruments, cheap music and a leader with little experience. The above receipts have been in use for many years and never failed in a single case to produce the results as given. There is nothing helps a town more or that its people will contribute so liberally to the support of, as a good band; but no intelligent community will do much to support an inferior one, and they cannot be blamed much in so doing. I have started out to have an independent organization and not continually annoy the citizens for aid, consequently no beggars, kickers or snakes in the grass need apply. I intend to earn as soon as I can the required amount of money to uniform this band in complete suits of buckskin. A little strange, but why not? We live on the border, composed of border men, and led by a buckskin border man, known from Colorado to the British Dominion as Buckskin Joe. Interpreted would be the Arkansas City Border Buckskin Brass Band and Orchestra. In short, the "4-B" band.

PROF. E. J. HOYT

This brought a great response. In two weeks, I had a thirteen piece aggregation, with correts, clarinets, trombones, and bass and snare drums. By the end of the month, we gave our first concert to a large and appreciative audience, all uniformed in buckskin and coonskin caps. I then announced that we were ready to negotiate with managers on short notice for long or short engagements, anywhere.

We were soon playing at every kind of event—balls, picnics, even funerals. Quoting from a July issue of the Geuda Springs *Herald:* "One of the best features of the grand double-barrel celebration held in this city on the third and fifth inst. was the music rendered by the Buckskin Band of Arkansas City. We congratulate Arkansas City on the possession of this worthy combination of musical talent. The selections by Prof. Hoyt, the competent leader, were choice, and the rendition of the same splendid. Before leaving our city the members of the band marched to the residence of our deceased friend and fellow townsman, George Sherbon, and escorted the remains to the school house, where the services were concluded. That beautiful and solemn funeral dirge will long be remembered by our citizens and particularly by the bereaved relatives, who are grateful." But the laurels that reflected the greatest credit on our organization were won at the first annual muster and camp of instruction of the new Kansas National Guard held at Topeka that autumn.

[In 1855, the first territorial legislature had passed a long act of twenty-seven sections providing for a militia. This was the "bogus legislature," elected by the votes of Missourians, and the actual residents of the territory refused to be governed by it. In 1858, the first free-state legislature amended the act, providing for a military board to take the matter out of the hands of the territorial authorities, which were friendly to slave power. The act was vetoed by the governor, but passed over the veto. Soon after Kansas was admitted to the Union, a thorough reorganization of the militia was effected, and the state divided into two districts, separated by the Kansas river, the number of brigades in each district to be directed by the governor, who was commander-in-chief by virtue of the constitution. During the Civil War, very little attention was given to the organization or its discipline. Practically all the men subject to service were mustered into the United States army "for three years, or during the war." In 1865, with the end of the war obviously near, another act was passed providing for the compensation and discipline of the troops. This remained the military law of the state until 1885.

[By the act of March 7, the militia, for the second time, underwent a complete reorganization, and the name was changed to the Kansas National Guard. The reorganization was commenced in April. All who did not desire to remain as part of the new guard were mustered out; new companies and regiments were mustered in; rules and regulations were adopted; and the state made one military district under the command of a major general, with four brigade districts, each under the command of a brigadier general. The major general and four brigadier generals were to act as a military board. The act also provided for an annual muster and camp of instruction, and the first was held at Topeka from September 28 to October 3, 1885.

[The Topeka *Journal* stated, on October 1: "The Kansas National Guard is still in camp.... Yesterday morning was spent in drilling by squads and companies until the grand parade was called. The National Guard then turned out in full force, thirty-two companies, and marched at the head of the immense column. After the parade, the troops were ordered out in battle. The battle was the feature of the day and the troops displayed much bravery, as well as exhibited the splendid discipline to which they have been subjected.... On tomorrow, the day will be devoted entirely to the instruction of officers and troops under the direction of Capt. Jacob Kline, of the Eighteenth Infantry, U.S.A. On Saturday, it is officially announced, camp will be broken and the troops will return to their respective homes....

["As the JOURNAL special car was whirled into the grounds at 7 o'clock this morning, the force was received with honors by the Scott Rifles, headed by the Buckskin Band of Arkansas City. The Scott Rifles, under the command of Lieutenant Alf Brant, were drawn into line as the car stopped, and stood at present arms, while the band, under the direction of their leader, 'Buckskin Joe,' the famous war-scout of the 49th New York Volunteers, played a number of selections. This band is oddly costumed in suits of buckskin in regular frontier style, and attract much attention with their clothes as well as their music. The reception and serenade was appreciated."]

Between band engagements, I built a large gymnasium in Arkansas City, equipped for all different exercises: horizontal bar, parallel bars, horizontal and diagonal ladders, expansion bars, flying rings, sand bags, dumb bells, and knotted ropes, trapeze and pullies. For light gymnastics: wands, light dumb bells, and swinging stirrups.

I opened my new hall Tuesday evening, June 30, 1885, with the attendant publicity as follows:

HEALTH, STRENGTH AND ELASTICITY

No more sleepless nights, no more consumption, no rheumatism; no round shoulders, no weak lungs or sallow complexion. Health and beauty are more valuable than gold. No spectators admitted during regular exercises. STUDENTS: Attend to it while you have a chance. It is just as necessary for you to look to your health as to your education. What is one without the other? You sit at your desk day after day, with your breast drawn in, lungs compressed and spine bent. What is the result? Consumption, weak lungs dyspepsia, crooked spine! Of what good is education with the loss of health and form? One course of Gymnastics will straighten you up, expand your lungs, straighten your crooked back, give brightness to your eyes, color to your sallow cheeks, and you will feel and look like a different being. You could then study and retain what you learn, and have a form like an Adonis. MERCHANTS, BOOKKEEPERS, CLERKS AND PROFESSIONAL MEN: You, too, need Gymnastics. Look at your puny, weak limbs and hollow chests. You can change them to strong, healthy ones if you will. LADIES: Don't turn up your pretty little noses, and say, "Ah weally I caunt be so hawrid, I am so delicate. What if my dear Chawls should learn that his pet was getting rosy cheeks—hawrid!" Silly as this sounds, there are those insipid, would-be delicate beings who think that to be pale and narrow contracted in body is to be refined and pretty. Sad delusion! Do you, young ladies, think that any sensible young man would take unto himself such a partner for life? Not he! Give him a bright-eyed, rosy-cheeked lass, with a form that any lad might envy. You will lay out hundreds of dollars for ribbons, laces, diamonds, paints and artificials to make you pretty in the eyes of your "expected," when one or two courses of Gymnastics would add more to your beauty than thousands of dollars worth of artificials and finery—to say nothing about the benefits of health, which is invaluable.

Within a few days I had all the gentlemen and ladies classes I could handle. I also used the new hall for dances and concerts up until the spring of 1886, when Arkansas City experienced a great "boom."

Already the town had felt the first urge brought on by the railroad. Mule-drawn and horse-drawn trolley cars became the modern method of transportation down Summit street, and Joseph Ranney [a native of Michigan who had moved his grocery business career west to Kansas] soon opened a new wholesale house [the Ranney-Alton Mercantile Company, later Ranney-Davis] in a big stone building at the corner of First street and Fifth avenue, the only establishment of its kind between Arkansas City and Gainesville, Texas.

We still represented the edge of the frontier. Oklahoma still was Indian country. The wide open spaces of western Texas remained to be settled. Most of the company's early business was supplying goods to Indian traders, boomer parties going into Oklahoma, and to wagon trains headed south across Red River.

A search for oil and gas around Arkansas City began about this time, but most all the first oil drilling efforts wound up as small gas wells or dry holes. Today oil derricks dot the countryside in every direction from the city, and the wealth they bring in has spread through the entire community. I remember the first test was put down by an oil operator from Pittsburgh, Pennsylvania, on the west bank of the Walnut. He drilled to 1200 feet, and found gas at 800 feet but no oil. The well was plugged, but gas continued to seep from below the plug, and skaters on the Walnut, which iced over in the winter, used to light the gas to illuminate their night skating parties.

The town was plagued with bachelors at that time. There were about twenty among our leading citizens who took part in social, business and public life, and caused no end of anxiety among the feminine population. None of them, I am happy to say, became middle-aged. The charming girls of the period charmed and won them. Many a romance began with those skating parties on the Walnut. My oldest daughter, Ella, was married to one Eddy Blubaugh in the spring of '86, and Clara, my next oldest, married Billy Parker, a cowpuncher, in the fall of '87.

Clara left me to set the time of day for her wedding, so I announced it would be at sunrise. I further requested that, before the ceremony was performed, she should step into the back yard and allow me to shoot an apple off her head at thirty paces. This was done, and more too. She put an old-fashioned matchbox on her head, and I put a bullet through it in the same manner. She still considers it a great relic.

I then asked Billy to step up and have his nerve tested, but he could not be persuaded. I said, "I only wanted to show you the kind of mettle you will have to contend with."

Ella always held my objects for fancy shooting. The most dangerous was the "scalp shot." This was to shoot a penny held sideways by a spring wire on her forehead, then turning to give me a side shot, I would shoot off the wire.

This "boom" business naturally raised real estate and other prices to heights unknown in any city outside the oil fields and gold camps. My father came down from Canada and invested in considerable property. A couple of sharks got to him and were about to clean him when I discovered their trick, saving him several thousand dollars. One went crazy over their great loss and committed suicide. But it set Father back in the old notch again.

Then the "boom" suddenly subsided, leaving most of us practically broke and asking each other, "What started it?"

One fellow, who lost everything, went berserk and rushed through town with a shotgun, firing a shot through the window of a woman's house into a baby buggy. The mother had just removed her child from the buggy, and its life was saved. Then he made a mad rush south into an alley. Another man ran down the alley to stop him, only to get a charge of buckshot in the side of the neck, killing him instantly.

The officers took after the assassin, and he fled from town, taking a stand behind a straw stack in the bottoms. A few shots were exchanged before I arrived on the scene. He had always been a good friend of mine, and I walked up to the stack and persuaded him to surrender before they killed him with their rifles.

We took him back to town and placed him in jail under heavy guard. A lynch mob planned to capture the armory at Thompson's barn, seize all the militia's guns, and take over the situation. Thompson got word to me at midnight. I jumped to the door in my shirt tail, blowing my bugle long, loud and strong, and in ten minutes the whole company was in line and marching to the rescue. The fellow got a long term in prison, but was pardoned seven years later, after his old mother nearly lost her mind and spent all the money she had getting him out.

I sold my gymnasium that winter and began traveling around the country doing object shooting. I could hit anything I could see, moving or stationary. Eddy Blubaugh went with me, and would hold any object I desired, in any position. Shooting ashes from his cigarette while smoking was routine, and I could throw 50 glass balls into the air with my own hands and break them with actual bullets fired from my .44 Winchester carbine in two minutes time by the clock. I also played the cornet in a theater to help keep the wolf from the door.

Then my wife came down with pneumonia and we had a 21-day siege of it. Then Ella gave birth to her first child, Ruby, and Belle came down with the lung fever again, and we had another 21-day siege.

This was the spring of 1888, and I had decided to break up housekeeping and take both my sons-in-law and families to the Rockies, when I received a message from Major Gordon W. Lillie, the famed "Pawnee Bill," to come to Wichita. Lillie had just organized a great Historical Wild West Exhibition and Indian Encampment, with Charles M. Southwell, of Philadelphia, as general manager, and wished to engage me as a performer and my full buckskin-uniformed band to play the music.

I left for Wichita at once, and received the surprise of my life. The moment I walked into the hotel, a man stepped up behind me with, "I say, Yank, if you have coffee to trade for 'baccy, we can make a dicker." I hadn't heard that voice since the night I helped storm the Rebel fort above York River during the Peninsular Campaign of 1862, but I recognized it immediately. I whirled and clutched the hand of my one time enemy with whom I had exchanged shots in the moonlight—William Palmer of Texas, "Butcher-knife Bill."

Lillie and Southwell were forgotten while we renewed our acquaintance. Palmer had returned to the western country after the war, driving cattle to Kansas trail towns and working on Texas ranches. During the Indian wars on the plains, he had scouted for the army. After that, he had spent several years hunting in Colorado and the Rockies, but somehow our trails had never crossed. Later, he heard I had been killed at White River during the Ute massacre.

The previous fall he had come to Wichita and laid claim to an island in the Arkansas just below the Thirteenth street bridge. He had spent the winter trapping along the river, and although the country was thickly populated, found it reasonably profitable. He had built himself a tepee on the island after the style of the Indian, and few people had any idea he was a citizen of the place until discovered by the Pawnee Bill combination searching for talent.

He had declined their offer, he told me. "I've quit the wild west forever and want to rest in peace." But we stood and talked over old times until a large crowd had gathered to listen; a reporter overheard our conversation, the next day the papers carried the story of our experiences on the frontier, and Palmer agreed to join us.

On March 31, I contracted with Lillie to furnish my band

at $450 per month, and returned to Arkansas City to organize. We were to report to his ranch at Wellington, where his special show train, with 165 buffalo, horses, mules, and broncos; 84 Pawnee, Kaw, Wichita, Comanche and Kiowa Indians; 50 cowboys and Mexicans; and 30 trappers, hunters and scouts, waited to start to New York as soon as orders were received from Southwell. Our destination was Belgium, where Lillie had a guarantee from King Leopold of $3000 per week and expenses for six months at the Grand Exposition to be held in Brussels.

Then came a cablegram announcing the death of Emperor William, and the trip had to be cancelled. This left the show in the hole, for Lillie had several thousand dollars of printed matter to throw away and had to get out new billings for this country to play our way East. We opened at the new exhibition grounds in Wichita on May 10, and in midsummer arrived in Philadelphia, still in the hole.

Lillie couldn't understand it. On a whole the weather had been favorable; we got a great reception at St. Joseph, in Kansas City we played a whole week, and in Indianapolis, the newspapers commented on the general excellence of our show. We had one setback. At Columbus, Ohio, we got in jail. It was this way: At the evening show a couple of fellows came along outside the high fence and pelted the audience on the open seats inside our grounds with rocks. One of our cowboys went up on the top seats and ordered them to stop. They commenced to abuse him, and he pulled his six-shooter and killed one of them. Then things got lively. The police tried to enter our grounds, but we stood them off with our guns until the management persuaded us to let them in to find the man who had done the shooting. We let them inside, and they arrested all of us. We put up a big howl, and I don't think anyone within five blocks of the jail got any sleep that night. The next morning they lined us up in a big hall. The only clue they had was the dead man's companion who had witnessed the shooting, but he couldn't identify anybody, and they were obliged to let us go. Several had to pay fines for disturbing the peace, but it didn't cost the show anything. It was just that the money wasn't coming in as expected. At Pittsburgh, Lillie had to wire Southwell for enough money to get the show to Philadelphia.

We played at the Gentlemen's Driving Park in Philadelphia. It was here I aided a young lady in distress and netted the show a great deal of publicity. I will quote the story as it appeared in the press.

"Yesterday when Pawnee Bill's Wild West was playing at the Gentlemen's Driving Park, Miss Annie Harris, who has been educated in Germany, and resides at Ninth and Filbert streets, attended the exhibition.

"She is a plump, black-eyed girl of only 18 years, and on the performance closing, late in the afternoon, became separated from her escort and found herself alone in Belmont Glen as the shades of night were closing around her. A little frightened of the darkness and anxious to reach her home, the young girl was hastening along the path, when suddenly two men sprang from the bushes and seized her arms. Miss Harris struggled desperately for freedom, but all to no avail.

"'Let me go, gentlemen. Please let me go,' she entreated.

"The ruffians made no reply, and more vigorously than ever strove to drag her into the bushes. Then she shrieked piercingly and called:

"'Help! Help'

"At the girl's loud shriek for aid a muscular figure sprang into the path. Buckskin Joe, the famous Western scout, had heard her cries and was coming to her rescue. He took in the situation at a glance. One powerful blow shot her most formidable assailant into the rivulet that winds along the ravine, and a second later he had the fellow's companion by the throat and was choking him into unconsciousness. For a moment the two struggled, and then the scout rose from the senseless form of his antagonist and took Miss Harris' arm.

"She clung to him even after they had entered the cars and overwhelmed him with gratitude when he left her at her door."

Daily thereafter she haunted the Wild West grounds, and when we moved across the river to Gloucester, she followed me

158

there. I told her I had a family in Kansas, and advised her to go home.

On Monday, she visited the show again. This time she carried a letter for me and was seeking a messenger to deliver it. Her glance fell upon the brawny figure of "Captain Stubbs," a Chief of the Kaw Nation, whose Indian name was Wah-Ki-Kaw, or "Gift-Giver."

Stubbs was the dude of our camp. He wore countless silver amulets. He was decorated with yards of bead circlets, his rusty silk hat was bound by a crimson scarf, and gay ribbons streamed from every part of his clothing. He was nearly 40 years old, his face was painted a vivid yellow, and his straight black hair hung like a storm-stricken mop about his head. To him Miss Harris gave the tender missive.

He pretended to deliver it, but actually made no attempt to find me. Instead, he returned in a few minutes to feast his eyes on the paleface maiden's charms. He began an ardent wooing with the impetuosity of a prairie fire, and though he could only say "How" and "Big Injun stuck on white squaw," Miss Harris soon saw that he loved her from the depths of his aboriginal heart.

When she came back on Tuesday, she inquired no more for me. The charms of Wah-Ki-Kaw had erased from her mind the face of her dashing rescuer, and she cared only for the dude of the Wild West show. On Wednesday, she consented to become the bride of her Indian lover, and they were wedded by the simple ceremony of joining hands, and pronouncing, "How! You my squaw!" "You my husband!"

Wah-Ki-Kaw immediately fulfilled the promise of his name. He presented all the articles of his personal adornment, including two ponies, to friends in camp. But he avoided me like a plague. He was jealous of me, and announced his intention of leaving with his squaw for the reservation of his tribe on the Arkansas without delay.

Lillie [who never lost an opportunity to capitalize on the least publicity] told him that, in order to have everything in accordance with the law, he would purchase him a marriage license and have a grand solemnization of the affair at the close of Thursday's performance. The next afternoon, thousands packed our grounds to witness the event. The ceremony was performed by a Justice of the Peace, and afterwards performed by Pawnee Bill according to the Indian custom. As present-making was the main feature of the latter, everything was given away from pie and lemonade to an Irish jackass, followed that evening by a wedding dance and a feast at which the show's pet dog was sacrificed.

After that, people went wild over Pawnee Bill's Wild West. We played five weeks at Gloucester Beach. Over 150,000 persons passed through our gates, the newspapers proclaimed it "the most realistic illustration of Wild West life ever attempted," and there was no sign of a let-up in popular interest as we toured south. The Bennett family of sharpshooters and Annie Oakley, "Little Sure-Shot," a former attraction with Buffalo Bill's show, had now joined us.

We played at fairs mostly, but Lillie lost money because of poor contracts with fairgrounds people. Then the rains set in. I suggested we turn back where we had established our popularity, for I knew what early fall weather in that part of the country could do to small circuses. But Lillie and Southwell scoffed at my idea. The rains cut attendance and drained our small treasury. As my boys had not been paid in two months, I cancelled our contract with the show and returned home to Kansas and disbanded.

Lillie and Southwell went on without us, playing small towns and trying to recoup their losses. Bad weather continued. In October, at Easton, Maryland, they ran into a sheriff with an attachment for their livestock and equipment, and had to petition the citizens for enough money to send the Indians back to their reservations.

CHAPTER XIV

The Oklahoma "Land Rush" of 1889—
Appointed Deputy United States Marshal—
I Organize My Own Wild West Show, and
Take a Claim in the Cherokee Outlet

About this time, Arkansas City began experiencing its second big "boom." The entire border was undergoing a great change. Early in 1886, the Santa Fe railroad had decided to build across the Indian country toward Texas. The bridge over the Arkansas River had been completed in September of that year. By November, one accommodation train was running to Ponca, a little station in the Cherokee Outlet. By January, 1887, this service had been extended to Cow Creek, a half mile south of the present town of Perry, and in February, reached Deer Creek, now Guthrie. From there the tracks were laid south through the present sites of Edmond and Oklahoma City. Meanwhile, the Gulf, Colorado and Santa Fe was building north from Gainesville. On April 26, 1887, the two roads joined at Purcell, on the South Canadian River, 154 miles south of Arkansas City. On April 19, 1889, a depot was completed at Guthrie. The agitation by boomer colonies in the surrounding states and their representatives in Washington had caused Congress to declare the unassigned, central part of this territory open to settlement on April 22, and every person who was 21 years old could file on a 160-acre farm. Homeseekers along the Kansas border had only to cross the Outlet to reach the north boundary of the Oklahoma lands, but thousands coming from the northern part of the state stopped in

Arkansas City, Caldwell, and Hunnewell before proceeding to replenish their supplies. Stores sold out of provisions many times before this transient population dwindled in mid-April, and afterwards, the towns became main supply points for the new territory.

The credit for getting these lands opened has been given to the great boomer leaders like Captain David L. Payne, Captain William L. Couch, Samuel Crocker, Sidney Clarke, and Major Lillie, who came back after his show failed in Maryland and headed up a huge colony organized at Wichita. These men deserve the laurels, but there were hundreds more, seldom mentioned, who did as much behind scenes.

The plan adopted, I must say, was a daisy. The "run" was at noon. The starting signal was to be given by shots from the rifles of United States cavalry troops who guarded the borders. An estimated 100,000 persons came from the east, west, north, and south to claim 1,888,900 acres. They stood in line three days under a red hot sun, ankle deep in dust, without food or water, waiting for the crack of the gun to see who could get there first, and then were obliged to defend their claims with shotguns, rifles and six-shooters. I had seen buffalo stampedes on the plains that shook the earth, but they were nothing compared with this stampede for land. They even had to beat the Santa Fe, which amassed much passenger equipment at Arkansas City and ran it in 12-car trains to Guthrie. The first train carried 1,000 passengers. The next ten carried enough to bring the total to 10,000. The people leaped from the cars, all wild with excitement like the first battle of Bull Run.

Tent cities sprang up overnight. My son-in-law's father, Dave Blubaugh, of Winfield, was one of the first to stake a lot on the capitol site at Guthrie, and erected the first eating house and hotel. The day of the run it was a tent; a few days later it was a wooden structure. Eddy himself lost his life the opening day in a fracas. We picked him up dead alongside the railroad track. That is all we knew about it. His wife gave birth to a baby boy five days later, on April 27, and named him Vance Joseph Blubaugh. Belle and I took the child to raise, and he is still with us—Vance Joseph

Blubaugh Hoyt. My close friend, Captain Couch, also made the run and staked a claim in Oklahoma City. He was elected the town's first mayor and served with honor until April 14, 1890, when he was shot and killed by a trespasser.

Most fights and killings that occurred were the result of land squabbles. But there was much other lawlessness to contend with. Fakirs, bunco-steerers, and professional crooks of all kinds were there to dip their hands in the homesteader's purse, and vicious outlaws, many of whom traveled in organized gangs, came for no other purpose than to live off the land. For more than a year there was no government and no authority to establish one. The towns set up provisional governments to protect themselves against these elements, but generally the country operated under federal statutes that were applicable. Finally, Congress passed an act organizing it as a territory, dividing it into counties and providing for a full complement of executive, legislative, and judicial officers. President Harrison signed the bill on May 2, 1890.

The unoccupied Cherokee Outlet was under the jurisdiction of the federal courts of Kansas, and on March 10, 1890, I was appointed federal deputy under R. L. Walker, the United States Marshal for the District of Kansas, at Wichita, to help clean up this country. My old friend, Butcher-knife Bill Palmer, was deputized as my posse. We maintained our headquarters at Arkansas City, and worked mostly the area west and south of the Osage Nation, through the Ponca, Nez Perce, Otoe, and Pawnee reservations to the Cimarron. The first brush we had was with a gang of horse thieves in the hills near the fork of the Cimarron and the Arkansas. Strongly fortified, they stood us off one day and night, when government troops from the Pawnee Agency came to our assistance, and they evacuated and fled the country out of our jurisdiction.

The Dalton boys and their cohorts were the most dangerous outlaws operating at that time. They were a gang of train robbers who had sprung up over in the Indian Nations and also were wanted for train robbery in California. On May 9, 1891, they held up the Texas Express on the Santa Fe near Cow Creek in the

Outlet, and fled east toward the Osage country. Palmer and I took down the Arkansas, thinking to intercept them, but never found a trace. For weeks we rode in several posses that chased them all over the territory while the stories of their exploits and reward notices for their arrest and conviction filled the newspapers. Months later, the gang was wiped out by armed citizens when they attempted to rob two banks at Coffeyville.

Much of our work was apprehending government timber thieves and whiskey peddlers. I remember once having scouted the country and starting back when we met a fellow with a big load of wood and a team of poor horses.

I asked, "Where did you get that wood? Certainly you never got it in the Outlet. That would be violating the law."

"You must have hauled it from the Kansas border," Palmer suggested.

"No," said he, "I got it on Turkey Creek."

So we had to arrest him. While we were unhitching his team, he told us a pitiful story of how his family was depending on that wood to keep from freezing and living on half rations in the struggle to make a go on their claim.

So seldom did we find such an honest man that I told him to take the wood and get to hell out of there. But I made him promise not to cut any more timber in the Outlet.

It was different with whiskey peddlers. I had no sympathy for them. While the selling, transporting, and possession of liquor in the Indian Nations and on Indian reservations was prohibited, saloons were legal in Oklahoma, and whiskey runners flourished all along the border. We landed several in jail at Guthrie and Wichita. I always figured they could find an honest way to make a living.

Which brings to mind the time we were coming out of the Outlet and found an old mother skunk with two kittens. We captured her and cut her musk bag, then put all of them in a gunny sack and brought them home. I put them in a cage, but the old skunk escaped one night, leaving her kittens. I had an old cat that had just lost hers, and put her in the cage, and in no time she was nursing them as if they were her own. In fact, she raised them. It was a comical sight to see those two skunks after they were half grown following her around. Everyone thought the cat had given birth to them, and I never told anybody different. My little grandson used to sit on the front porch and play with them, and people would stop and stare in wonderment.

One day the groceryman came to our house with some potatoes, and I sent him down in the cellar. He dropped his basket, and up he came, shouting, "Joe, Joe, there's two skunks in your cellar!" Down I went, catching one of them by the tail, and ran after him, throwing the skunk on him. You should have heard him yell and run for his life. It was great fun for little Vance.

One evening in March, a special was received from Washington stating that the Cherokee Outlet had been declared public land and open to settlement under the homestead laws and that bona fide settlers would not be disturbed. The news spread like a prairie fire. Men and women ran into the streets shouting for joy and gesticulating wildly. More than a hundred who had been holding disputed claims in Oklahoma mounted horses and pressed every mode of conveyance into service and started for the Outlet. Then it was announced that it was all a false alarm, and Palmer and I received orders from the United States Marshal to go down and move them out.

We rode 35 miles that night, and about 10 o'clock the next morning we reached a choice spot where several of these families were camped with covered wagons. We rode up and asked what they were doing there, and a half-dozen burly fellows came forward and told us, "We are goin' to take up this land."

"Well," said I, " it is all a mistake, and you will have to get out."

"Wal," said the spokesman for the group, " that is too damned bad. I reckon we'll stay anyhow."

"You won't stay alive," said I. "You have until 1 o'clock to pack and move."

Palmer and I rode off a little ways from the camp, checked our rifles and six-shooters, and sat down behind some trees to wait.

At 1 o'clock we rose in position, leveled our guns at the camp and told them to move. It was a difficult thing to force our own friends off land they had fought so long to occupy, but we had a job to do. "The first man who reaches for a gun," I said, "will be shot."

The women commenced to cry and beg their men to hitch up. In a few minutes they had everything packed and ready, and we escorted them back to Kansas.

It was the last trip I made for the government. When I got home, there was a stranger at my house, waiting for me. He introduced himself as Mr. Boyden, manager of Crescent Park, at Providence, Rhode Island, and stated he had come all the way from the East to arrange for a strictly Wild West show to play at his great resort during the summer.

"I am tired of would-be Wild West shows and performers," he said, "and you have been highly recommended as a competent man for this work."

I told him I wasn't interested, as a show would be hard to organize that late in the season. But he insisted. He stayed with me five days, and promised to furnish me all the capital necessary to accomplish the undertaking.

So I turned the marshaling business over to Palmer, and went at it, selecting all the thoroughbreds I could find for the occasion. Within a few weeks I had a full complement of bronc riders, ropers, cowgirls, bucking horses, wild steers, and equipment, including an Overland Mail coach and an entire Indian village. This was not a peaked tent or two, artistically daubed by some modern artists, as had been seen in the many so-called Indian villages or encampments, but a bona fide *Pete-haw-e-rat* village— wigwams or tepees complete with their lodge-poles and trappings, purchased in the Indian Territory—illustrating the modes of living and the habits of the red man in his western home. Here the public could actually see the squaws at their bead work, making moccasins, sewing wampum, tanning hides; the braves in council smoking the peace pipe, or playing with their chieftain's young; and not the least attractive, the merry-faced papooses that never cried, but, strapped to a board, were truly objects of great interest. It became one of the leading features of our exhibition.

The music was furnished by Reeves' Great American Band, which played in the park at night after each afternoon's performance. I also conceived the idea of introducing a novelty Ox-Horn Band composed entirely of my family, so I searched the country over for the largest Texas cow and steer horns I could find. These were cut to form a chord—alto, bass, etc. On these horns, my daughters Ella, Clara, and Flotina, my wife Belle, and my son-in-law Billy Parker played the on and after time to my aria on the cornet. When in full swing, it sounded like a steam calliope.

We shipped our wild and woolly outfit by special train to Providence, and thousands gathered to witness our arrival and march seven miles to take the boat for Boyden's Park, the "Coney Island of the East." Many things had been added since I last visited the place after leaving the Pawnee Bill show: French carousel, aerial flight, Russian toboggan, bowling alley, a mammoth dancing pavilion. And the famous "shore dinners" were more deserving than ever. Amidst all this, we set down everything from the western ranges and corn fed—Buckskin Joe's Realistic Wild West.

We were hot stuff, you bet. We opened with a parade of the entire outfit and introduction of characters. This was followed by a horseback quadrille, a cornet solo, and novelty numbers by the Ox-Horn Band. I had two old Canadian Indians with me, White Eagle and White Cloud. Their election as chiefs was very attractive, and the attack by their wild tribes on my cabin by night was sensational. Then came an Indian war-dance, Indian foot-race, Indian girl's foot-race, an Indian's chase for a wife, an attack on the Overland Mail, Pony Express ride, hanging a horse thief, roping acts, and bucking horse and wild steer riding, climaxed by the capture and re-capture of an immigrant child, played by my three-year-old grandson, whom I dressed in a buckskin suit of his own and billed as "Buckskin Joe, Jr." In the attack on the wagon train, the child was the only survivor, and the Indians would carry him off to burn at the stake, but he was saved by the cowboys who rushed shooting and yelling through the smoke to the rescue at the psychological moment. Then I would gallop up, cut him loose from the stake, stand him on the horn of my saddle, and race away across the arena to the wild applause of the excited audience.

The first day we opened, we gave three performances, and Boyden banked nearly $10,000. He could hardly believe it, and it was far beyond our expectations. We had a great season and lots of fun, like the afternoon one of our cowboys, Sam Hamlin— "Locoed Sam" I called him, because he was always full and rode a locoed horse—took a notion to ride up into the grandstand. It was a sight to see all those people rolling off their seats, the pitching bronc, and Sam spurring him all over the place, jumping him over the railing and back to the ground again, then dashing away at a breakneck speed.

Another afternoon a couple of my Indians, who had been drinking, got to fighting. I stole their six-shooters, then had my cowboys rope and tie them down until they were sober.

One night, Locoed Sam and some of the boys got hilarious in the dancing pavilion and commenced shooting up the place, Western style. Boyden got frightened and rousted me out of bed, yelling, "Joe, Joe, for God's sake stop it!" I rushed through the dark to the scene, arriving in time to calm them down and prevent some of the wildly fleeing natives from getting killed.

Despite these incidents, we were liked by all, and that winter, everything was shipped back home safe and sound with plenty to eat and rum to wash it down. The day my grandson and I parted company with my Indian chiefs at St. Johns, Canada, old White Cloud said, "Me no more see little Joe and Joe Buck. No More. We meet in the happy hunting grounds sometime. Goodbye, Little Brave and Big Brave."

When I reached Arkansas City, I found a "tent" population of nearly 75,000 people. The town's banner year for population and business was 1893. The government had decided to open the Cherokee Outlet to settlement. As in 1889, stores sold out of provisions many times before the population decreased early the morning of September 16, the day of the opening, and left the place almost deserted.

Again the time was at noon, and thousands congregated on the state line under a scorching sun in dust ankle deep, waiting for the same old signal—the crack of a gun.

Palmer and I were mounted on fine horses, and off we dashed 21 miles inland to a beautiful prairie on the Salt Fork of the Arkansas that we had crossed many times during our expeditions as federal marshals. Palmer was so elated upon reaching the location that he leaped off his horse, drove his stake and danced around it and howled like an Indian.

Several others took claims around us. Someone fired the prairie to check the main body of the rush, and a good many suffered death and lost all they had. We had to constantly ride over our land, armed to the teeth and ready to fight to hold it. Those two claims, each worth $10,000 today, cost us only a paltry few dollars and a good chance to be killed little more than two decades ago.

CHAPTER XV

Gold in Honduras—My Adventuring Days Are Over

I spent the next three years attending my real-estate interests in Arkansas City and proving up my claim in the Outlet, stock-raising, and farming. I also operated the largest apiary in that part of the country. I bought everything I could find treating on bee-culture, Palmer helped me, and I soon had over forty stands going. I sold all the honey they could produce and made good money. But when the new gold discoveries in Alaska caused the great rush to the Klondike in 1897, I struck the adventure trail again.

Some mining men in the East engaged Palmer and myself to do some prospecting. We had the option of going to the Klondike or Central America, and choosing what seemed the least of the two evils, we prepared to ransack the unknown interior of the latter.

On February 26, 1898, after securing a complete camping outfit and other necessities, we took passage on the steamer *Oteri*. This steamer was a combination freight and passenger boat in the service of the United Fruit Company, making trips between New Orleans and the chief ports of British and Spanish Honduras. On the morning of the fifth day out, the *Oteri* anchored in the harbor of Belize. Leaving Belize harbor, she circled the coast southward, stopping only once ere she anchored at Trujillo.

The moment we landed our troubles began. The Commandante at the customs house promptly relieved me of my rifle, which I had been using to shoot sharks on the way over. He also seized our gear, claiming heavy duties. With the aid of the American consul we got our freight through free under the Mining Act, but the Commandante became fascinated with my .40-82 Winchester and begged me to sell it to him. I finally let him have it for fifty *pesos*, which was better than nothing, for in that country anything that resembled a Winchester was politely taken on one pretext or another. As we had other rifles, together with five revolvers and plenty of ammunition, hidden in false bottoms and partitions of our trunks, our loss was not heavy. I hated to part with that rifle. It was a beautiful weapon, one I had used in the Wild West shows, and I felt sad about it the rest of the day. Toward evening, however, I was somewhat cheered.

We were strapping up our luggage after it had been overhauled from end to end, when there came a loud report, followed by the noise of splitting wood and a series of yells that sounded like hyenas fighting. Rushing to the custom office, I arrived in time to see several of the natives flying head-first out the windows. The old Commandante stood in the center of the room, his face blanched and eyes popping from their sockets. I knew what had happened. I had left a cartridge in the rifle. The Commandante, in examining the workings of his new-found treasure, had exploded the charge, tearing a huge hole in the wall.

The next day we met Alamondo, our *mozo*. His arrival brought our number up to six, the Eastern members of our company joining us here being Bert Dare, Charlie Rowe, and a Doctor Howard. Our party was now complete, and we immediately began to pack for the trail.

We purchased eight pack-mules and two horses—a small pony named Tom Thumb and an old horse called Bolivar—to aid us in our fight with the mountain trails, dense forests, miry swamps, wild beasts, reptiles, and tribes of Spanish-speaking, uncivilized Indians. We did not buy mounts for ourselves, but trudged at the sides of our pack animals on foot, as everyone did in that country. The food they carried was the most important thing in that part of the world, where the odds were ten to one against survival.

We had mapped our course directly south from Trujillo, through Jutigalpa, to Vijao, a small native village in the Olancho Department, situated on the borders of what, perhaps, was the wildest country on the face of the earth. From there we were to leave for the unknown and plunge deeper into the mountains and jungles until we had penetrated as far south as Nicaragua. Gold, we had been told, was to be found in this south-central region, silver in almost all sections, and that only 5 per cent of the existing mines in the country were being worked. This particular region was practically unexplored. Finishing our work here, we planned to retreat to Jutigalpa, and from there travel northwest to La Pimienta, at which place we could take the interoceanic railway to Puerto Cortez, some sixty miles distant, traveling thence back to the States.

On March 18, we left Trujillo with twelve-hundred pounds of freight, taking a mere mule-path that wound before us over a veritable sea of precipitous mountains and jungle- and forest-choked valleys. We took our time, careful not to over-tax our animals or ourselves in the early part of the journey, saving our strength for what lay beyond.

The heat of the sun was almost unbearable, and the higher we climbed, the more oppressive and sultry became the air. We soon realized we had a good deal to learn about the country, but, being old-timers at such tasks, Palmer and I had made greater preparations than the others. We knew from our Colorado experiences the bad effect of glaring sunlight on the eyes, and had brought a dozen pair of colored glasses. We lost no time putting them to use. The glare was so blinding that looking up the trail was like looking at the reflection of a mirror.

But we had yet to learn what time of day was best for travel. By 2 o'clock in the afternoon, the rays of the sun found their way through our shirts and blistered our backs; the animals were barely able to drag themselves under their loads, almost prostrated by the heat; and we were forced to make camp after crossing the first range. Later, we discovered it was really the foothills of greater heights beyond, waiting to be conquered.

After tending our pack train, Doctor Howard set to work applying soothing lotions to our backs. Luckily for us, he carried a small stock of drugs, as well as surgical instruments, for the trip. There was no such thing as a physician in this benighted land, and whenever we camped near a village, our *mozo* would tell the natives about our wonderful doctor. They would come from miles around, bringing their sick, and Howard never refused to do anything he could for them. We admired him for the man he was, and during the trip he saved the lives of each of us many times. He was the handiest fellow I ever trekked with.

Weary from our day of difficulties, we swung our hammocks early. Sleeping on the ground at night was not healthful, for the malaria mosquito was ever present. The natives knew the insects had something to do with the disease and slept in mud huts with windows and doors tightly closed. The heat inside was roasting, but they didn't seem to mind the temperature. We preferred our hammocks and protective netting.

We were back on the trail at daybreak. We had learned our lesson the day before. We traveled until 10 o'clock that morning, then spent the rest of the day in camp.

For ten days we continued to force our way deeper into the wilds, following old trails, making them where there were none, often cutting a path through the matted undergrowth. Many times our track was in precipitous places where a misstep or slip would have sent man and beast to eternity.

The eleventh morning out we entered the most difficult jungle we had so far traversed. We were in a large valley, covered with all sorts of tropical trees and large plants matted together with vines. It was horrible stuff to cut through, and often we had to crawl between as best we could. The ground was swampy, in places liquid mud—black, fetid, and oily. At every step dozens of insects darted into our faces and viciously avenged themselves for our intrusion. They stung like bees and it was impossible to fight them off. Snakes crawled under our feet and hung from the growth above. Many were the exact color of the vines, which caused us to advance cautiously. Great fungi and monstrous, oozy slimy plants hung in festoons about us, covered with horrid-looking tree-toads and other loathsome creatures. As we forced our painful way onward, the damp, offensive exhalations from the earth struck upon our lungs like fumes of nitric acid, and each breath seemed to bear the menace of yellow fever. All the while the sun beat down, making that nightmare of vegetation like a hothouse.

Our animals were becoming faint from the effluvia. Now and then one would stop and lick the slimy ground in hope of finding something to quench its thirst, then look up pitifully and move on, with its tongue hanging out, panting like a dog. Finally, Bert Dare fell prostrate, overcome by the heat. "Oh, God!" he moaned. "I can't stand it any longer." Howard and I remained with him while Palmer and Rowe and the *mozo* kept cutting a way out.

We worked with poor Dare until we were dizzy from fatigue and he was past the danger mark. We were too weak to carry him, so we forced him to walk by holding him up and pushing him on. The heat was appalling.

We soon caught up with the others, but it was another half-hour before we emerged at the foot of the next mountain range. The *mozo* took us up a small gulch, where we made camp beside a streamlet that trickled down into the inferno we had just come through. Making steady progress, we camped a few days later on a low, timbered plain with mountains to the south. Just before sundown I discovered an old deserted hut in the woods, and proposed that we sleep in it for the night.

The *mozo* promptly objected. "No, no, Don Jose! There is a devil in the hut."

"Well," said I, "we'll just sleep there anyway." But the others agreed it was not good judgment to take risks that even a native declined.

So I questioned the *mozo* about the old adobe. All he knew

was that the place had not been inhabited for nearly sixty years. According to all accounts, stray natives who had slept upon its floor had been attacked by some powerful "thing" just before daybreak and in most cases terribly mutilated. No one ever discovered what it was, and everyone passed the cabin at a distance, muttering to themselves, "Mucho diablo."

"If there is a devil in there, I am going to make his acquaintance," I said, and rose from the camp fire and began to buckle on my cartridge belt.

Alamondo fell on his knees before me and began to mutter a short prayer. As I was examining my revolver to make sure every chamber was loaded, he took a little red sack from around his neck and asked me to carry it with me, that it would keep the "devil" away. I had no belief in such charms, but to keep him faithful, I put it in my pocket. Then, bidding the others good night, I took my blanket and made for the cabin.

I had a little difficulty opening the door. Inside, I took a candle from my belt and lit it. I was in a low, musty-smelling room that looked as if it had not been occupied since the days of Noah. The puncheon floor, full of holes, laid across old sleepers. The whole cabin was built of split logs, plastered over with mud. There was a large niche in the north wall that served as a window. Under this stood an old bunk, and I selected it as my resting place for the night. I blew out the candle and looked through the niche in the wall, and saw the *mozo* building up the camp fire, the native custom for keeping wild animals away.

Stretching my weary limbs, I wrapped in my blanket and was soon lost in sound sleep. It must have been after midnight that I was suddenly awakened by something walking on the loose planks of the floor. Slowly I gripped the butt of my Colt, my finger encircling the trigger, ready for action, and breathlessly awaited the intruder's first move.

The noise continued along the far wall. It didn't sound like an animal. It walked like a man, for I could hear only the tread of two feet. Carefully I drew myself up on my left elbow and peered into the darkness toward the opposite side of the room. I stared

176

until my eyes ached. Then, suddenly, I heard heavy breathing above me and felt my blanket slowly slide from my grasp. Something was climbing up over the foot of my bunk! Looking down quickly, I saw two red eyes coming toward me, staring like balls of fire.

I pulled the trigger, and my revolver spat flame and roared!

It would be impossible to describe what happened next, for I do not know myself. What I heard was the most hideous shrieks and screams that ever grated on my ears; there was a rush, a scramble, then something sprang over my head and out the large niche in the wall. I could hear a cracking of the bushes outside, then all was still.

I sprang to the window to see what I had hit, and saw the rest of the party, guns in hand, running toward the cabin. The *mozo* had snatched a pine knot from the fire and was bringing up the rear.

I opened the door, and by the light of the torch, we saw a furry object lying outside. As I stooped to examine it, Alamondo seized my arm and jumped back in fright.

"No, no, Don Jose!" he shrieked. "Come away! Come away! Halingo! Halingo!"

I lifted the animal's head with my foot, and convinced the *mozo* that it was dead.

I had never seen such a creature. It would have stood five feet high, belonged to the ape family, and resembled a man more than anything. These animals are a brownish color except for their faces, which are white. They walk erect on their hind legs, and the males possess a long white beard, giving them a frightening appearance. The female carries her young in her arms like a woman. The interior of Central America is their habitat; I do not know if they are found elsewhere. They seldom appear in the daytime, are ferocious when cornered, and have the strength of a dozen men. The natives regard this man-monkey as an evil spirit, and call it the "Halingo."

On the fourteenth day we crossed the Negro River and camped near a small village called Manto. This was the largest stream we had crossed to that point, and we had great difficulty landing our animals safely on the other side.

Two days later we crossed the most formidable mountain range we had encountered, and at the peak of the rocky trail, old Bolivar made a misstep and went rolling and tumbling a thousand feet into the jungle below. Pots, pans, shovels and sluice-forks flew every direction. We scrambled down the mountain. Doctor Howard was first to reach him.

Bolivar lay on his back in a creek, squirming and kicking like a trapped pig. Palmer and I caught him about the neck, all hands closed in, and we were able to remove the pack from his back. When we let him up, he jumped half around, looked up the mountain, and gave a mighty snort, as much to say: "Great Scot! Am I still alive?" He was alive all right, but injured badly, and died that night.

The morning of April 15, we descended to a large plateau in view of Jutigalpa, a village of 3,000 inhabitants and the largest in the region. Two centuries before it had fallen to the conquering Spaniards, and the graves still there, enclosed by a stone wall, bore witness to those put to the sword. We went into camp here and rested two days, then crossed the great Guayamapa and took the trail to Vijao.

About 3 o'clock in the morning of our third camp, I was awakened by the whimpering of our animals and the heavy tread of a beast outside our tent. Snatching up my revolver, I started to investigate, when Alamondo leaped headlong into the tent and fell at my feet. The rest of the party awakened just as some monster thundered past the entrance. Then followed such snorting as I had never heard.

Palmer and I rushed into the open. Before us were the dark bulks of two animals, stamping our fire and flinging the brands in a frantic manner. Then they made a rush for our pack mules, which were tugging at their ropes. Palmer and I fired the same instant. But we had aimed at the same beast, and only one of the marauders crashed to the ground. The other whirled and charged us.

We barely had time to jump from its path, delivering two shots apiece at the hurtling beast's ribs, which, somehow, failed to take effect. There was a hideous squeal, ending in a reverberating roar. The brute dashed past and plunged into the center of our tent, taking canvas, ropes, pins, and all in a mad charge through the jungle.

I heard a human scream, and realized that one of our party was still in the tent. I rushed to where the tent had fallen from the brute's back, slit the canvas, and out crawled Charlie Rowe, so badly scared his teeth chattered.

"Are you hurt, Charlie?" I asked.

"N-no," he stuttered. "W-what was it—a cyclone or tornado?"

I didn't know myself. Somewhat vexed by the slowness he had shown at a critical moment, I asked, "What kept you inside so long?"

"My revolver got mixed in my blanket," he replied. "I was looking for it when the quake hit."

Palmer and Dare came up, and as we started gathering the heap of torn canvas to drag it back to camp, I stumbled on another form. I cut another hole and uncovered our *mozo*. I felt for his pulse, but found none. Quickly we carried him to Doctor Howard, but it was no use. Blood oozed from his mouth, and his chest had been crushed. The brute had trampled him badly. Alamondo was dead.

Curious to know what kind of beasts had attacked us, we built up the fire. The one killed lay a short distance away—a slate-colored, pig-like animal, with a long, flexible proboscis and fierce looking head. Its hide was thick and tough, its feet three-toed, its ears like a burro, and a tail like a mule.

We learned that this was one of the most dreaded animals in the interior, because of his frequent attacks on wayfarers. A fire to them is like a red rag to a bull—they will always charge it, stamping it out with their feet. They are very destructive and, being large and clumsy, often demolish whole fields of native corn. They travel in the nighttime, along recognized trails, which peculiarity enables the natives to trap them easily. At the foot of the trails, the Indian hunters plant dozens of sharpened sticks, pointing upward. As the brutes thunder down the mountain sides in the darkness, they impale themselves on the stakes and perish. *Tapirus terrestris* is the scientific name for this creature. The natives call it the "Danto."

The next morning we buried poor Alamondo, covering his grave with large stones to protect it from jungle beasts, then, sorrowfully, moved on without a guide. Fortunately, we were not far from Vijao. We arrived in the little village of 500 inhabitants that afternoon—the end of our trail.

Here we met William Buell, the only white man in the country at that time. Buell seemed happy to receive us, and gave us much valuable information on mining possibilities in the region. He owned a mine nearby, from which he had accumulated a fortune. In fact, he liked the place so well he had married a native woman and made it his permanent home.

He furnished us a diving suit, for we were to prospect the rivers as well as the Dipilto Mountains, the richest mining region in Central America—I might add, in the world. He also purchased our mules and pony, for we had no further use for them, there being no trails ahead for animals to tread. Our supplies and equipment were to be packed on the backs of carriers, who could be secured at 25¢ per day. The dynamite we carried ourselves, for the natives were great thieves, and explosives were scarce.

The last day at Vijao, some of our tools were stolen. This provoked us, for everything we had brought in was needed. There was no place to purchase new picks and shovels. But the new *mozo* we engaged soon informed us who had stolen the tools and directed us to the thief's hut.

The fellow wasn't at home, so we sat down and waited. Presently he appeared on the trail. Palmer, who possessed a hasty temper as well as a gigantic body, curtly informed him the purpose of our call. Of course, he denied it. This did not please Palmer, and his temper got the best of him. Quick as a flash, he poked the native in the ribs with the muzzle of his revolver.

"Produce them tools in a hurry," Palmer told him, "or I'll kill you pronto."

The native stood staring, as if not understanding what he meant. Suddenly Palmer lifted his revolver and fired it beside the man's ear. With a frightened yell, he sprang through the door of his hut. The terrified thief refused to show himself again, but a moment later, our tools came flying out the door, one by one.

With twenty carriers, packing between them fifteen-hundred pounds of freight, we broke camp for our fifty-mile march through the deep jungles that lay ahead. Again we found forests that were almost impenetrable because of the steaming heat and rank vegetation, but in five days we had established a permanent camp on the banks of the Julan River, where no white man except Buell had set foot before, and sent our carriers back to Vijao.

We kept our *mozo*. With his help, we built a log cabin on a small knoll in the center of a clearing. The rainy season sets in about the middle of May and lasts six months. This gave us a few weeks to get settled. We built a high log fence around the cabin, mainly to keep away the wild hogs that seemed bent on sleeping beneath our windows and grunting all night. Next, we captured a couple of young bulls and tamed them for draught purposes. We built a cart, and used this to carry ore from an old shaft we had discovered. The shaft had been worked by Spaniards in the early days, and looked promising.

To cut a long story short, we spent four years in these mountains, working the rivers and our old Spanish mine. It proved to be one of the richest in Central America. We filed on the discovery at Jutigalpa, to give us mineral rights to the land we were on, and during the second year of our stay, had a portable steam stamp-mill packed in, which we obtained in Chicago. The quartz was free milling and ran six ounces to the ton, while the vein was over four feet in width. Our dreams were coming true—we were swiftly becoming rich. But life has many downs, and it finally fell like a thunderbolt.

For purposes here, I will call the man "Mr. Z," as he had been forced to leave the States, owing to a major crime, and is today a prominent citizen of Tegucigalpa, the capital of Honduras, where he had taken up residence and married a native woman.

Some time prior to our arrival in the country, he had secured from the President at Tegucigalpa several large concessions. One included a mineral lease to all lands lying between the Julan and Guayamapa. It also stipulated that he was to have all old Spanish concessions between these rivers which had reverted to the government. The ancient shaft we were working was one of these reverted concessions, and about a year after our machinery was installed and we were turning out bricks of gold, Mr. Z appeared and informed us that we were trespassers.

I produced the papers that had been issued at Jutigalpa, and informed him the taxes had been paid to date. His reply set our brains awhirl: our papers were only from the capital of the Olancho Department in which we were mining, while *his* papers had been signed at Tegucigalpa by the President of the Republic.

Palmer and I immediately made a trip to Jutigalpa. The officials evidently were expecting us, for they told us the same story. I asked if they were in the habit of issuing two leases for the same tract of land and receiving taxes from both parties. They said they had made a mistake that could not be corrected now, as one of the periodical revolutions was under way, and we would be lucky to get out of the country alive. Moreover, if we did not give up our mine at once, we would be turned out by the militia.

This was too much for Palmer. He shook his fist in their faces and told them to try it, that we had plenty of ammunition and knew how to kill. We were both veterans of the Civil War, he added, and had served as Government scouts during the Indian outbreaks in the West. It would .be easy to fight them if they attempted to attack us. We then hunted up the American consul and explained our circumstances. He admitted that we had a good case against the government, but doubted we could do anything in the face of the current revolt.

So we returned to camp—and were greeted with another sorrow. During our absence, Charlie Rowe had died with the fever. Howard and Dare had buried him in front of our cabin at the foot of a pole on which waved the American flag.

A few weeks later, a squad of soldiers visited us. Armed with revolvers and several belts of ammunition, we met them at the gate. The captain served us with orders to vacate the premises. I told him we had papers giving us a right to the land, and that we stood under the protection of the flag that waved above us.

"If you wish to open fire under those conditions," I said, "we are perfectly willing. Our party is not large, but our guns are loaded."

They did not fire, but held a brief council among themselves and finally departed. There was no assurance, however, that they would not come back.

Things went along nicely for six months. Then one morning Mr. Z, with more than a dozen armed natives, came out of the woods. We met them, prepared for the worst.

He told us we had twenty-four hours to get off his land. "If you have not cleared out at that time, I will order my men to attack."

Before I could answer, the hot-blooded Palmer shouted, "Why in hell waste all that time? We're not leaving our mine. If you want a fight, let's start it now!"

Mr. Z reached for his revolver. Before he got it out of the holster, Palmer fired, and two of Z's men fell. The natives fired back, killing the lion-hearted Doctor Howard. Then we opened with a volley, which claimed another four of them, and the rest fled for the jungle like scared rats. Mr. Z stood alone like a statue, his face as white as a bleached bone and revolver still undrawn. Palmer leaped for him like a mountain cat, his huge fist shot out, and Mr. Z went sprawling down the slope. He scrambled to his feet, cursing viciously and swearing vengeance, but he lost no time bolting into the jungle. Palmer stood and laughed.

I turned back to the beloved Doctor Howard, who lay dead at our feet. As I did so, a sniper's rifle cracked from the timber. I felt a sickening pain dart up my right leg, and I collapsed to the earth in agony. I had been hit just above the ankle, and wondered, as I lay there crippled, if the end had come.

There were only three of us left—four including the *mozo*, who was our friend to the last. What sort of fight could we put up against the authorities of the Republic of Honduras—to say nothing of the fever, the wild beasts, and Mr. Z? We had killed six natives, the revolution was on, and Mr. Z had sworn vengeance. He possessed a great deal of influence, and would never rest until he had driven us out or killed us. What should we do? There was only one answer—go at once.

Sorrowfully we dug another grave under the flag of the country I was now longing for, and laid the doctor to rest beside Charlie Rowe, whose life he had struggled in vain to save.

Then we bade farewell to the old camp that had been our home four years. We knew instinctively we should never return. Our beautiful stamp-mill, erected with so much trouble and expense, would rust to ruin; the fortune that had been almost in our grasp was only a dream. We took the few gold bricks we had made with us—only $3,000 worth in all. Our expedition and machinery had cost $10,000, so our loss was heavy.

Slowly we moved down the trail into the jungle. I rode one of the bulls, while Palmer, Dare, and the *mozo* walked by my side. Each step the bull took gave me intense pain, and I cared little whether I lived or died. The big trek of my life had been a failure.

Dare left us at Vijao. He had no desire to return to the States, for he had no close relatives living, and William Buell took him in. We also bade farewell to our *mozo*, for we had no further need of his services. Palmer and I were headed for Puerto Cortez, and there was a trail all the way.

We bought two mules and started for Jutigalpa, the nearest place I could receive medical attention. For over 500 miles I rode a mule, fording some twenty streams and rivers with my foot held above my head to keep the filthy water from poisoning the wound, and all the time gangrene was threatening to eat my leg away. I have often wondered how I endured it.

At Puerto Cortez, Palmer told me goodbye. He was a born wanderer, he said, and wanted to do some prospecting in Mexico.

On May 27, 1902, I landed in New Orleans, with a crutch under my arm and able to tell the tale of four years of purgatory in the most uncivilized land in which I had ever tried to survive. I was happy to reach home.

Dare died of fever in Vijao less than a year after I left him. Palmer, my old partner, died of typhoid in Mexico City a few years later. In 1909, I disposed of my interests in Kansas and Oklahoma and moved to California to enjoy the beach-life and sunshine, and settled down to being something of a hard-headed, one-horse philosopher.

Seventy-seven years I carry upon my shoulders, but I am still tough and active, and Central America is a wonderfully rich mining country. Some day I may go down the western coast and penetrate into its interior once more. Who knows? The lure of gold is all-powerful, and I often feel myself longing for the wilderness again.

Index

187

Index

190

Index

Miles, Agent John, 109
Miles, Colonel Nelson A., 109, 111
Milk Creek, 132
Milks, Ezra, 113
Miller Brothers, 88
Milton, Nova Scotia, 145
Minimic, 108
Minneapolis, Minnesota, 86, 100
Missisquoi County, Vermont, 71
Mittson, Peter, 15–16
Monitor, 51
Mountain Maid, 71
Mowry, Al, 112–113
Mowry, Henry, 113
Mt. Orford, 1, 78
Murray, John H., 78

McCall, General, 43
McClay, Jack, 141–142, 144, 146
McClellan, General George B., 39–41, 46–47, 49–50, 52, 58–59, 64
McDonough County, Illinois, 82
McIntire, George H., 113
McKinley, Ben, 88

Negro River, 177
Neil, Lieutenant Colonel Thomas H., 110
Nelson, George, 113
New Athenaeum Theater, 125, 127, 130
New Orleans, 171, 185
New York City, 63, 65, 78, 87
Newport, Vermont, 71
Newport News, Virginia, 51
Newton, Mollie, 130
Nez Perce reservation, 163
Nicaragua, 173
Nichols, J. S., 112
Nichols, Professor, 26
No-po-wa-lee, 95–96
Noonday Lode, 141
Norfolk, Virginia, 35
North Enfield, New Hampshire, 67–68, 79, 81
Norton, G. H., 92–93, 112–114

Oakley, Annie ("Little Sure-Shot"), 160
Occidentals, the, 121
Odonivan Racer Lode, 128
Ogdensburg, New York, 74

Oil Creek, Pennsylvania, 33
Oklahoma City, 161–162
Olancho Department, 173, 182
Old Gutch, 102–103
Old Hundred, 44
Old Shippy, 21, 23, 25
"Old Uncle Pete," 122
Olympic Theater, 122
Osage Agency, 105
Osage Indians, 92–96, 119
Osage Nation, 163
Osborn, Governor, 111
Oteri, 171
Otoe Reservation, 163
Ottawa, Canada, 72
Ottawa Indians, 93
Ottawa River, 72
Ouray, Chief, 132–133
Ox-Horn Band, 167

Palmer, William ("Butcher-knife Bill"), 54, 156, 163–165, 169, 171–173, 178–185
Panama, New York, 30, 33, 37
Parker, Billy, 154, 167
Parker, Quannah, 108
Parlour Circus, 72
Patterson, A. W., 113
Patterson, General, 36
Paus, the Dutch Lepetre, 122
Pawnee Agency, 163
Pawnee Indians, 157
Pawnee Reservation, 163
Payne, Captain David L., 162
Pearson, Peter, 101, 113
Pearson's Hall, 102
Pedestal Contortion Act, 122
Peninsular Campaign of 1862, 40, 156
Peppers, Tom, 88–89
Perry, Oklahoma, 161
Philadelphia, Pennsylvania, 38, 77, 118, 156–158
Phillips, John, 113
Pidgeon Hill, Vermont, 71
Pitkin, Frederick W., 132
Pittsburgh, Pennsylvania, 34, 36, 153
Platte River, 117
Ponca Reservation, 163
Pope, General John, 64
Portsmouth Grove, Rhode Island, 65
Potomac River, 36, 39, 41, 49

Index